MONEY
MOMENTS

MONEY MOMENTS

SIMPLE STEPS TO FINANCIAL WELL-BEING

JASON BUTLER

To Uncle Dave and Auntie Molly,
who taught me about working and saving

ISBN-13: 978-1979914208
ISBN-10: 1979914206

First published in the United Kingdom in 2017 via CreateSpace
Published by J&J Butler Consultants (UK) Limited,
44 The Pantiles, Tunbridge Wells, Kent, TN2 5TN
Copyright © 2017 Jason Butler

For further information please visit www.jason-butler.com

Book Design: Sheer Design and Typesetting

CONTENTS

MONEY MIND
THOUGHTS, FEELINGS AND PERSPECTIVES

CONTROL OVER DAY TO DAY FINANCES

MANAGING YOUR MONEY, NOT YOUR MONEY MANAGING YOU

CAPACITY TO ABSORB A FINANCIAL SHOCK:

BEING ABLE TO COPE WITH THE UNFORESEEABLE

FINANCIAL FREEDOM TO MAKE CHOICES TO ENJOY LIFE:
BEING ABLE TO AFFORD NEEDS, WANTS AND TO BE GENEROUS

BEING ON TRACK TO MEET YOUR FINANCIAL GOALS:
CREATING AND UPDATING A FINANCIAL PLAN

WALKING THE TALK:

TIME TO TAKE ACTION

ACKNOWLEDGEMENTS

Writing is a solitary activity. I formulate the concept, gather the research and draft the text on my own. But along the way and as the final book comes together there are lots of people who make a valuable contribution.

I am very grateful to Simonne Gnessen of Wise Monkey Coaching, who generously reviewed the first draft and made several suggestions for improvement, drawing on her extensive money coaching experience. Chris Budd, the financial well-being expert of Ovation Finance, made useful suggestions on the structure and format.

Thanks also goes to Claer Barrett and James Pickford at the Financial Times for believing in me and taking a punt to see if I could write about personal finance for FT Money. I am honoured to be in the company of so many other talented and distinguished writers and contributors.

Many thanks to my production team: Tony Triggs for his forensic eye for detail and candour; Nigel Sutherland for his brilliant cartoons; Megan Sheer for her beautiful book design and typesetting, and Georgia Kirke at Write Business Results for her advice and guidance on self-publishing.

A massive thank you to the ever resourceful and adaptable Amy Hyland who hands all things digital and marketing, including my website.

Thanks to Michael Lightfoot of Aquila Heywood, for being the unwitting inspiration for writing the book.

Thanks also to all my financial services friends who provided information, insights, ideas and material including Robin Powell, Pete Matthew, Abraham Okusanya, Andy Hart, Andrew Hallam, Alan Smith, Paul Armson, Steve Caps, Tina Weeks, Ian Brewer, Lien Luu, Jonquil Lowe, Tim Morgan and Holly MacKay.

FOREWORD

Having picked up this book you might be thinking to yourself: "I'm not the sort of person who would read a book about money."

Before you put it back on the shelf, consider this.

If you're "not that sort of person" (and let's face it – who is?) then this book is *exactly* what you've been looking for.

If you would like to have a better relationship with money, then you need to start thinking about that relationship emotionally. You don't need to be a maths wizard with a huge calculator. You need to work out how you *feel* about money, which is very different.

The good news is that Jason's book provides you with an easy, fast and enjoyable way to explore those feelings.

And, for most of us, the feeling will be a mixture of fear, anxiety and even depression. We spend more of our lives worrying about money than anything else. This is usually because we're worried we won't have enough to make it to the end of the month.

A lot of this boils down to the fear of making a decision. What savings account should we get? What energy supplier should we choose? How do we join a pension? How can we budget to put some money aside every month?

As Jason says, the fear that we might make the *wrong* decision means we usually end up making *no* decision. And in the long run that's often worse.

Jason is very different from most financial experts. He's made mistakes – and he's not afraid to admit it. He's splurged when he should have saved. He let a bad experience with maths at school colour his attitude towards money for years, thinking he could never be good with money if he couldn't do algebra and trigonometry. And, later in life, he kept chasing money without properly considering what truly made him feel happy and fulfilled.

But making mistakes is important. It's how we learn.

Jason overcame these mistakes and he learned from them. Reading his stories – which tackle everything from student loans to the finances of cohabiting and planning your retirement savings – you can learn from them too.

As Jason says, believing that you *can* be good with money is the first step.

When we first met – over a cup of coffee in the Financial Times canteen – Jason told me he wanted to write a monthly column for the FT exploring the emotional relationship we have with money.

"I've never written a column before, and let's face it, I could be crap at it," he said. "But I really want to try."

I don't need to tell you that his column has been a huge success. Jason talks about money in a different language – and it's a language that you'll understand and relate to.

Whether you're rich, poor or (like most of us) somewhere in between, money is a taboo subject. We don't like talking about it. And when people do they often don't tell the whole truth.

We all have a friend on Facebook who makes us feel envious by constantly posting pictures of their exotic holidays, flash cars and new clothes. You might think, "Well if she can have that, I want it too!" But all too often, as Jason explains, these show-offs are funding their apparently swanky lifestyles by getting deep into debt. The reality is that they could end up paying for these things several times over when all the interest is added on.

Another way we find it hard to tell the truth is by saying "I can't afford it." These four little words can make you feel like a failure – particularly if your children are the ones asking for the unaffordable things! We want to have enough money to keep our families happy. But saying yes all the time won't make them happy. It will just make them want more things.

I'll let you into a secret. Debt is easy to come by as the big banks and financial services companies can make a hell of a lot of profit by selling us easy access to our dreams.

If a 21 year-old borrowed £3,000 on a typical credit card deal, and only made the minimum repayment each month, they would be nearly 50 years old by the time they cleared the debt – and would have paid nearly £4,000 in interest on top of the £3,000 they originally borrowed.

Of course, the credit card companies will never make this clear when you apply. That 'small print' is small for a reason. Just because everyone else is doing it does not make it okay. It's up to you to work out whether it's a good deal or not.

And this is where Jason's book can help. He explains things very clearly, without the jargon that the financial services industry uses to bamboozle us. Dipping into the little lessons in this book will give you the confidence to ask questions when you are faced with similar choices, and to help you find some answers about what drives your own relationship with money.

You might feel that you're "crap" with money. But put that thought to the back of your mind. Armed with this book, you can change all that. The only thing you require? The same desire as Jason – to really want to try.

Claer Barrett
Personal Finance Editor, Financial Times

INTRODUCTION

What's important about money to you?

It's a simple enough question but answering it is far from easy.

Money, the means of exchange which allows our society to operate, is a tricky thing and most people have a complicated relationship with it.

- How much money is 'enough'?

- Are you spending money on things that make you fulfilled and happy?

- Do you have money worries, problems or anxiety?

- Do you judge your self-worth by your net worth?

- Do you feel you are in control of your personal finances?

These are common questions that arose throughout the 25 years I was a financial adviser.

Money has consistently been found to be one of the biggest causes of stress and anxiety, often leading to relationship breakdown, poor health, worker absenteeism, and unhappiness.

Individuals are constantly bombarded with messages telling them that happiness is having more and better 'stuff' and that materialism is the route to fulfilment.

People are living longer, the world of work is rapidly changing and the financial choices people are faced with are becoming ever more complex.

The cost of living continues to rise and many people face the prospect of a lifetime of financial struggle.

Owning a home is a pipe dream for many young people, who also face having to work for longer than previous generations.

But despite today's challenges, I firmly believe that it is possible for most people to live a fulfilling and purposeful life, whatever their level of income or wealth.

Human well-being comprises five elements[1]

- **Career** (how you spend your time);

- **Social** (relationships and love);

- **Physical** (good health and energy);

- **Community** (engagement with where you live); and

- **Financial**

This book is a collection of stories and insights which can help you to improve and maintain **financial well-being**.

The best definition I've found to describe financial well-being is as follows:

'Financial well-being can be defined as a state of being wherein a person can fully meet current and ongoing financial obligations, can feel secure in their financial future, and is able to make choices that allow enjoyment of life.'[2]

Financial well-being can be broken down into four key elements which are shown in the table below.

THE FOUR ELEMENTS OF FINANCIAL WELL-BEING[3]

	PRESENT	FUTURE
SECURITY	**Control** over your day to day, month to month finances	**Capacity** to absorb a financial shock
FREEDOM OF CHOICE	**Financial freedom** to make choices that let you enjoy life	**On track** to meet your financial goals

There are several degrees of financial well-being or wellness, and these can be likened to a staircase as shown below, together with the percentage of UK households in each category.[4]

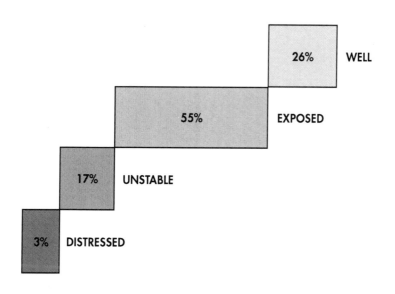

This book is my attempt to help you to have a better relationship with money and to adopt the habits and behaviours that will help you to be financially well, so that you can live the life you want.

Firstly, we explore how we think about money, the role it plays in our lives and identify some basic concepts you need to understand.

Then we'll look at each of the four elements of financial well-being through a number of real life stories. Each illustrates a key insight, concept, habit or mindset which academic research and my own professional experience suggests improves financial well-being in that area.

Do feel free, however, to read the chapters in any order, as each gives a valuable lesson in financial well-being.

Carry the book with you wherever you go and read it little and often, until your awareness and understanding are such that you feel more confident, capable and motivated to spend and manage your money wisely.

The last chapter has a simple financial well-being checklist to help you make positive and lasting changes and keep on track.

Don't forget that you aren't aiming for perfection but to maximise your life satisfaction and fulfilment, by using your money in a way that is in tune with your values.

The British-Irish painter Francis Bacon said 'Money is a great servant but a bad master.'

I want you to become master over your money so it can serve you: you can live your life to the full, free from money worries, anxiety and stress.

Now, let's talk about you and your money . . .

MONEY MIND

THOUGHTS, FEELINGS AND PERSPECTIVES

1

DUNCE OF THE CLASS

HOW SELF-LIMITING BELIEFS AFFECT YOUR FINANCIAL CONFIDENCE AND CAPABILITY

*'**Compound interest** is the eighth wonder of the world. He who understands it, earns it ... he who doesn't ... pays it. **Compound interest** is the most powerful force in the universe.'*

Albert Einstein

Maths was never my strongest or favourite subject at school.

However, the quality of teaching at both my primary and secondary school was pretty poor. At secondary school I would often put my hand up in a maths lesson and say 'I don't understand, can you please explain that again?'

Invariably the teacher would sigh, roll their eyes and say 'We have to move on Butler, keep up.'

I only met one maths teacher who ever made it fun and accessible and who bothered to explain concepts and ideas in ways that I could understand, and he taught me for just one term.

Over the five years that I was at secondary school, my confidence with numbers gradually declined to such a level that I dreaded maths lessons and just sat through them daydreaming.

Although I left school with half a dozen 'O' Levels (the forerunner to GCSEs), my grade in maths was one up from the lowest possible.

At this stage I told myself that I was no good at the subject and would never be able to grasp financial concepts and calculations.

I felt that I was destined to be a maths dunce all my life.

I entered the financial services sector completely by chance in a sales based role. But I quickly became frustrated and annoyed at my lack of mathematical ability and felt that if I was going to progress I would need to do something about it.

I enrolled on a basic maths evening class at a local college.

The tutor on that course was a breath of fresh air.

'Whatever negative thoughts you have about maths, forget them. After this course you will be better with numbers, you will feel better about mathematics and it will change your life,' said the tutor.

And he was right.

Gradually, week by week I learnt all the main mathematical concepts and principles which I'd never understood at school.

I started to enjoy maths and financial problem solving.

My confidence started to increase.

A few years later, when I decided to train to become a professional financial planner and investment manager, I realised that I needed to raise my mathematics skills to a much higher level.

I enrolled on a suitable weekly advanced mathematics night class.

The tutor was fun and highly engaging and stated that we were all perfectly capable of learning advanced maths, if we had a positive attitude, put in the work, and didn't give up.

I learned about the time-value of money, geometric mean, standard deviation, dispersion and a range of other advanced financial principles.

With the tutor's encouragement and enthusiasm I progressed rapidly and also became adept at using spreadsheets and a financial calculator.

Eventually I passed both my investment management and financial planning examinations and over the next twenty years built a highly successful career in financial planning.

While I don't enjoy mathematics as much as music, reading and writing, I no longer fear it and have a positive self-image about my financial capabilities.

Many people have self-limiting beliefs about money, numbers and mathematics which keep them from being better with their finances.

But self-limiting beliefs are not truths: they are just beliefs.

These beliefs are usually deep-seated and arise from childhood and our life experiences.

The key is to identify any self-limiting belief you have relating to money, understand how it arose, challenge it, and overcome it.

I refused to accept my poor mathematical capabilities, I did something about it and it changed my life.

You can too.

2

TWO MINDS

THE FINANCIAL TUSSLE THAT GOES ON IN YOUR HEAD AND WHAT TO DO ABOUT IT

'The test of a first-rate intelligence is the ability to hold two opposed ideas in the mind at the same time, and still retain the ability to function.'

F. Scott Fitzgerald, American writer

Many years ago I wanted to attend a big financial planning conference in the United States.

Money was quite tight at the time and I carefully weighed up the cost of the trip – both in terms of money and time – against the benefits.

After consideration I decided to go, made the necessary arrangements and planned the week's itinerary.

I was careful with my day-to-day spending and avoided staying up late drinking in the bar with other delegates.

One afternoon, just after the formal conference had finished, a few of my financial planning friends who had come with me on the trip, asked me to go with them to visit a large local shopping complex.

I agreed to go, even though I don't like shops or shopping.

We milled in and out of lots of different shops, until we ended up in an electronics shop, which sold mobile phones, headphones, cameras and music systems.

I started looking at the video cameras, which back then had a mini cassette onto which the video was recorded.

The sales assistant started engaging me in conversation, asking me what I was looking for in a video camera.

I told him that I was just looking.

He started to show me one particular video camera, pointing out features and benefits and how easy it was to use.

I commented that it seemed rather expensive.

His response was to show me a wide-angle lens which made the pictures even more amazing, which he advised he could throw in with the camera for only an extra $100.

Then he said something highly emotive.

'How can you put a price on capturing video of your kids when they are young? You need this camera.'

And that was it.

I got out my credit card and paid about $1,000 for the camera and lens, which 30 minutes previously I didn't know I needed or wanted.

I felt great about the purchase for a few weeks, until I received my credit card bill!

So why did I succumb to an impulsive purchase of an expensive and unnecessary item instead of putting that money in my retirement plan?

A key reason is because we have two modes of thinking, one instinctive and the other reflective.

Think of these two modes as a bit like having different financial personalities.

Richard Thaler and Cass Sunstein, two distinguished professors of behavioural economics describe these personalities as a far-sighted 'Planner' and a myopic 'Doer'.

The Planner represents the reflective thinking mode and the Doer represents the instinctive mode.

'The Planner is trying to promote your long-term welfare but must cope with the feelings, mischief, and strong will of the Doer, who is exposed to the temptations that come with arousal.

'Recent research in neuroeconomics has found evidence consistent with this two-system conception of self-control.

'Some parts of the brain get tempted, and other parts are prepared to enable us to resist temptation by assessing how we should react to the temptation.

'Sometimes the two parts of the brain can be in severe conflict – a kind of battle that one or the other is bound to lose.'[5]

Being aware of these competing personalities is one thing, but doing something to rein in your Doer is another.

The two most effective things you can do to put your Planner in control and resist your Doer's urges are to commit to a financial planning goal (for example saving £10,000 towards a future house purchase deposit) and leverage the power of accountability and our natural desire to avoid the pain of financial loss.

You do this by getting someone to monitor your progress towards your goal and acknowledge your progress.

And you should also agree some form of financial sanction if you don't do the things that you agreed it will take to achieve your goal.

The website www.stickk.com provides a simple framework and free tools to help people's Planners constrain their Doers and achieve any important goal.

Your Planner won't win every battle but hopefully it can now win the war.

3

IF YOU THINK YOU CAN

THE POWER OF SELF-BELIEF

'A good decision is based on knowledge and not on numbers.'

Plato, ancient Greek philosopher

I grew up in a very small terraced house in London with my parents and three siblings. We had no space, no money and few nice things or experiences.

During the long summer holiday one of my school friends asked me to come to spend the day at his house, which was about a mile away in a leafy, affluent area.

His house, which was down a long private road, was an enormous detached property set well back from the road.

The hallway was the width of my entire house.

They had a large games room with a snooker table.

They had tennis courts, a swimming pool and a large garden.

I was overwhelmed and felt very intimidated and inadequate.

After leaving my friend's house, as I walked back home, I reflected on the difference in our lifestyles.

Why didn't we have a comfortable house? Why did we have to live hand-to-mouth? Why didn't I have a garden to play in? Why did my parents work so many hours but always struggle financially?

I knew even then that being rich didn't necessarily make you a nice person, because the boy with the big house wasn't very nice but my best friend, who lived in a very modest house, was a lovely person.

As I walked home I resolved that when I became an adult I would not be poor and instead would have sufficient wealth to give me the freedom of choice to live a nice lifestyle, free from stress and worry.

I didn't know how I would achieve this outcome but, while I clearly hadn't fully developed my wider life principles and personal values, I had no doubt that I would be financially secure.

That early belief that I would not be poor has proven remarkably powerful in guiding me through various highs and lows to enjoy the freedom I enjoy today.

We all have different money perspectives, views and values, based on our culture, parents, education, peers, life experiences and personality traits.

Our deep-seated feelings about money can have a significant influence on our behaviours, habits and decisions.

The *theory of planned behaviour* was originally created by Icek Ajzen and links beliefs and behaviour.[6]

The theory explains that the more positive your beliefs and attitudes about money; the more you believe that good money behaviour is what others expect of you (the social norm); the more you have belief in your ability to adopt positive money behaviours and the better you'll be with money; and as a result you'll be happier.

Believing you can and will be good with money and have a fulfilling life is the foundation of financial well-being.

Whatever your current situation or your aspirations for the future, you *can* be better with money and reduce associated anxiety and stress. All you have to do is believe in yourself.

4

FACEBOOK FALSE

HOW PEER COMPARISON KEEPS YOU POOR

'Too many people spend money they haven't earned, to buy things they don't want, to impress people they don't like.'

Will Smith, American actor, producer, rapper, comedian, and songwriter.

A few years ago my friend Tim worked for a large company in South Africa.

Since the fall of the apartheid system in the 1990s, increasing numbers of black South Africans have secured higher paid jobs.

Tim got to know a black South African called Jimmy.

Jimmy was about 30 and had grown up in one of the poor townships.

Although Jimmy could read and write, he wasn't well educated and, when Tim first met him, Jimmy was working as a handyman for one of the large city hotels.

About a year later they met again.

Jimmy was wearing high-end clothes, an expensive-looking watch and designer sunglasses.

'Hey Jimmy, how are you?' asked Tim.

'I got myself a nice little job working for an insurance company for 300,000 Rand a year, replied Jimmy.

'Just bought myself a brand new Audi Q7,' he went on, smiling.

'That's great Jimmy, just make sure that you save some money for the future,' said Tim.

About a year later, Tim bumped into Jimmy again.

This time Jimmy didn't seem so upbeat.

'How's the job going Jimmy?' asked Tim.

'They laid me off and now I'm cleaning kitchens,' replied Jimmy dejectedly. 'I had to give the car back as I couldn't keep up with the payments.'

Tim's last image of Jimmy was seeing him drive off in a fifteen-year-old rusty red Toyota.

Jimmy, along with many newly affluent South Africans, had fallen foul of the mistaken need to flaunt material possessions as a sign of success and status. But material possessions did not bring lasting financial security and when his income stopped, so did the flash lifestyle.

Many people think that money gives them status, success, security, salvation or moral superiority.

Some of the things you could buy (an expensive sportscar) might confer a 'sense' of status, but never status itself.

Research finds that our happiness is affected by the extent to which we compare ourselves to others – a phenomenon known as 'social comparison'.

In one experiment people were given a choice of buying an experience or a possession.

The people who chose the experience faced less social comparison, which in turn improved their happiness.[7]

This makes sense because it is much harder to compare the emotional and pleasurable benefits arising from, say, a concert than, say, a new sports car.

If you recount an experience this will also make people like you more than if you talk about or flaunt your possessions (although constantly posting on social media pictures from your numerous holidays is unlikely to endear you to people).[8]

And comparing our income to others can also negatively affect our happiness.

In a US study, nearly half of the respondents said they'd prefer to live in a world where the average salary was $25,000 and they earned $50,000 than one where they earned $100,000 but the average was $200,000.[9]

Nearly half the people polled would accept half their income so long as they were better off than their peer group, family and neighbours.

In absolute terms this is a terrible deal but in relative terms they 'win'.

Social media often amplifies social comparison because it is pervasive and shows a curated version of how others want to be perceived.

Comparing yourself to others, particularly through material possessions, is a recipe for disaster when it comes to your financial well-being.

So avoid bragging about your possessions (in person or online) and take with a pinch of salt the materialism of others.

There is a good chance they are unhappy and up to their eyeballs in debt.

5

BALL AND CHAIN

WHY YOU NEED TO AVOID 'BAD' DEBT

---

*'Life is like an ever-shifting kaleidoscope –
a slight change, and all patterns alter.'*

Sharon Salzberg, author and buddhist teacher

Lorraine, Dave and their three teenaged children lived with Lorraine's parents.

Lorraine was the primary carer for her mum, who was seriously ill.

Her mum eventually died. and shortly afterwards Lorraine had a big argument with her dad which meant she and her family had to move out, into temporary accommodation.

'I got some help with setting up our new home but still had things I had to buy,' says Lorraine. 'Nothing fancy, just basics to make it comfortable for my kids. My only option was to use credit cards and catalogues.'

'Our place was in Woolwich and it was too far to expect them to walk each day [to Eltham]. But as the journey was less than three miles I wasn't able to get help with the fares.'

'Things just escalated from there. Then we were moved to Eltham. It was great to be near the kids' schools but it meant setting up a new home all over again.'

'Soon I was taking out loans to try and consolidate the debts, but the payments kept growing and I was left with no money to live off. It got totally out of control.'

'I went to a debt management company and ended up paying £500 a month, with a huge chunk of that going on admin fees.'

'Some of the debts were going down, but very slowly. And I was left with nothing to get by on.'

Things got even worse when Dave had to give up his job as a mechanic due to ill health, causing him and Lorraine to live apart so they could get the maximum State benefits.

'I'm a full-time carer for my youngest Christina, who is disabled,' she explains. 'It was awful not being able to live like a proper family. I was having sleepless nights and spent the whole time worrying and feeling sick.'

'We got constant hassle. Nasty letters and phone calls demanding money.'

'Lloyds TSB were the worst. They bombarded us with letters, calls at home and messages on my mobile. It was hell.'

After eight years, just trying to pay for the essentials, Lorraine and Dave ended up owing £30,000 on a bank overdraft, various credit cards, loans and a catalogue club.

Lorraine was at her wits' end.

'At my absolute rock bottom I felt like ending it all. I kept thinking if I was gone the debts would be gone, too, and the kids would be OK.

'That was the only way I could see out of this terrible mess.'

Lorraine eventually went to her local Citizens Advice Bureau for help.

The bureau's adviser explained the options available to Lorraine and Dave, including declaring bankruptcy.

As they were keen to repay their debts the adviser helped Lorraine draw up a budget and work out a debt management plan that they could afford.

Part of the plan included a freeze on debt interest so that all their monthly repayments reduced the outstanding debt.

The adviser also made sure they received all the State financial benefits they were entitled to.

After working out the plan with the money adviser Lorraine and her family got their lives back. 'We are all living together as one happy family and can see a day when we will finally be debt-free.' She said.[10]

Lorraine isn't alone in struggling with expensive unsecured debts which have been incurred to make ends meet.

In 2016 in the UK the Citizens Advice Bureau dealt with 350,000 people who were struggling to pay their debts, but they estimate that 2.9 million people in the UK are struggling with personal debt problems.[11]

We call the type of debt Lorraine had 'bad' debt because it is very expensive, relatively easy to obtain, usually incurred to fund spending and often difficult to repay.

Relationship breakdown, a fall in income due to job loss or illness, and unexpected expenditure are the most common things that lead to bad debt.

The practice of credit card providers automatically increasing credit limits, without the card holder's explicit request, encourages people to increase their borrowing.

Avoiding bad debt is essential to financial well-being.

While you can't control unforeseen events or circumstances that might adversely affect your financial position, there are things you can do to avoid accumulating bad debt.

It might sound simple but spending less than you earn when times are good should be absolutely central to your personal finances.

Building an emergency fund will help you to meet living costs for a while if you lose your job or have a fall in income.

Having sufficient income protection insurance will enable you to replace your income if you are unable to work for more than a few months due to illness or disability.

Make sure that you can afford any mortgage repayments if interest rates rise.

But if you or someone you know is struggling with debt you must face up to it. Do not bury your head in the sand and think it will go away; it won't!

It's perfectly natural to feel a range of emotions. Anxiety, regret, shame or fear are all common and normal – you are only human.

What you need to do is take control of the situation – don't see yourself as a victim.

Don't increase any existing credit facilities or take out any new ones to try to repay other debts – you'll just make the situation worse.

Write down what money you have coming in and going out and see if you can identify any ways to reduce outgoings that are *sustainable*, so you can stick with them.

Tell your creditors that you have a problem.

Prioritise paying your mortgage/rent and essential utilities before any other debts, no matter what other creditors say.

Open all the post you receive and get advice on how to deal with anything legal.

Check you are getting all the benefits to which you are entitled.

Work out how much you can realistically afford to repay creditors each month.

Once you have worked out a debt repayment plan you should then approach your lenders to get the interest frozen and agree how much you will repay each month.

If you are in the UK never pay for debt advice. Go to your local Citizens Advice Bureau, as they give free, independent, confidential help.[*]

Bad debt is like carrying around a really heavy backpack – it saps your energy, slows you down and eventually wears you out.

---

[*] In the United States there are a range of free or low cost credit counseling options provided by credit unions and nonprofit agencies. Make sure that they are accredited with either https://www.nfcc.org/ or http://fcaa.org/

6

DON'T LEAVE ME THIS WAY

WHAT CO-HABITEES NEED TO KNOW

*'I believe in large families:
every woman should have at least three husbands.'*

Zsa Zsa Gabor, Actress

Jeffrey Sharpe and Victoria McDonald had been a couple for many years and lived together with their four children in a home owned by Jeffrey. They had never felt the need to get legally married.

In 2010 Jeffrey died suddenly at the age of 31.

Because Jeffrey died without a will, his children were legally entitled to his entire estate, including the family home.

Victoria was entitled to nothing.

It transpired that Jeffrey also owned another property on which there was a small mortgage.

With help from family and friends Victoria continued to pay the repayments on the outstanding £54,000 mortgage as she wanted to retain it as a long-term investment for her children.

Victoria asked the lending bank to add her name to the mortgage, but they refused and demanded full repayment.

Eventually Victoria reluctantly put the property up for sale on behalf of Jeffrey's estate.

After dropping the asking price four times over the course of a year Victoria eventually accepted an offer of £110,000.

But the bank had already begun legal proceedings to repossess the property to enable them to dispose of the property to obtain repayment of their loan.

Despite the imminent sale, the bank was not prepared to wait for their money and continued to progress the legal proceedings.

If granted by the court this would see the property sold at auction, probably for less than the price Victoria had already agreed, plus Jeffrey's estate would have to pay the bank's legal costs.

Had Jeffrey and Victoria organised their finances differently, all of this could have been avoided.[12]

Cohabiting couple families were the fastest growing family type in the UK between 1996 and 2016, more than doubling from 1.5 million to 3.3 million families.[13]

In the UK cohabitees are not entitled to the same financial benefits as married couples. Capital gains and inheritance tax exemption, tax allowances and some state benefits are treated differently.

Cohabitees also have no automatic right to inherit any asset of a deceased partner, or guaranteed rights of ownership of an ex-partner's assets if the relationship ends, unless the asset was jointly owned.

A surviving cohabitee won't be liable for any debts owed by a deceased partner unless they were jointly owned.

Recent research by insurer Aviva found that three quarters (74%) of cohabiting couples aged 18-55 in the UK do not have a will, 64% have no life insurance, 33% have not named the beneficiary of their pension death benefits and only 4% have a written agreement in place to safe-guard against separation.[14]

Women suffer a higher degree of financial risk from cohabitation in the event of relationship breakdown or the death or illness of a male partner. This is due to a range of factors including longer life expectancy, higher unpaid caring duties leading to lower earning capacity, longer periods of ill health, and lower pension resources.

It makes a lot of sense for cohabitees to draw up a **cohabitation contract.**

This is a legal document which sets out how cohabitees' personal finances are to be handled during the relationship and, more importantly, how they will be dealt with if the relationship ends.[*]

Making sure cohabitees are joint owners of any bank accounts or other investments will enable each to continue to deal with these in the event of their partner's incapacity or death.

Each cohabitee should complete a nomination of beneficiary in respect of any pension death benefits.

Cohabitees should also draw up a will saying who gets what and who will be the legal guardian of any dependant children, as unmarried fathers or female partners of a deceased mother do not have automatic parental responsibility.[**]

---

[*] For a free cohabitation contract template visit: http://www.advicenow.org.uk/guides/how-make-living-together-agreement

[**] It is also possible to register parental responsibility in various ways without creating a will.

In the UK the Citizens Advice Bureau can give free advice and help to co-habitees. Their website has more details on the key points to consider.[15]

Getting married is still the simplest way cohabitees can improve their financial resilience through various tax benefits, state benefit entitlement and legal protection in the event of relationship breakdown, or the death or illness of their partner.

But if marriage doesn't suit, cohabitees should make sure they've covered the basic financial planning steps set out in this chapter to avoid a lot of heartache, hassle and expense.

7

LITTLE WORDS MEAN A LOT

WHY A STUDENT LOAN IS AN INVESTMENT NOT A DEBT

'If you think education is expensive – try ignorance.'

Eppie Lederer, American advice columnist and author

When my eldest daughter was in her first year of study for her 'A'-Levels we discussed the merits of her going to university.

While some young people need a degree as the foundation of their training, for example for careers in medicine or law, many do not.

For some young people a university education is a nice to have, not a need, particularly if they are not particularly academic.

Although I never went to university, I explained that most of the people I know who had gone felt that it was a very positive experience and highly recommended it.

A university education is, however, as much about developing as a person – becoming independent, meeting lots of different types of people, becoming self-disciplined – as it is about learning.

My daughter decided that she did want to go to university.

My daughter then said 'But dad, what about all the student debt I'll end up with? I can't face owing over £50,000 before I've even started work.'

I explained that the cost of her university education was not a debt like a mortgage or bank loan, but simply a way of the government quantifying how much extra **tax** she might pay from her future earnings.*

'You'll only start repaying the cost of your university education to the extent that you earn over a certain amount (currently £25,000 in the UK), It's not taken into account for mortgage purposes and no repayments are required if you stop work to have a family,' I explained.

'So it's really a graduate tax then, so that those who don't go to university don't have to pay for those who do?' my daughter asked.

'Yes, that's right.'

'Oh, I feel a lot better about it now I look at it like that. Well if I'm likely to pay higher tax in the future as a result, I need to do a decent degree at a top university,' she concluded.

So if you or someone you know are thinking about going to university, stop worrying about how much you might have to pay back out of your future earnings, and instead think about what benefits you might derive from the whole experience.

Little words do mean a lot so stop saying 'student debt' and start saying 'potential graduate tax if I earn enough'.

---

* The conditions of higher education loans in different countries will vary from the UK, and so this chapter might not be as relevant

8

CRY ME A RIVER

A KEY CONCEPT TO GRASP

'Good habits formed at youth make all the difference.'

Aristotle, ancient Greek philosopher and scientist

I recently gave a lecture to a large group of financial services under-graduates at a major UK university.

'Please raise your hand if you are a multi-millionaire NOT as a result of receiving an inheritance,' I asked.

Not one hand went up.

'I'm surprised we don't have any hands raised,' I said. 'Because most, if not all, of you here today are, in fact, multi-millionaires.

'While you might not have accumulated much, if any, financial capital, you all have an enormous amount of human capital on your balance sheet.

'Human capital represents the potential future earnings and wealth creation arising from exploiting your personal lifetime knowledge, talents, skills, abilities, experience, intelligence, training, judgment, and wisdom.

'Now, can I please have another show of hands. Who here is a multi-millionaire?'

Every hand went up!

This story illustrates that how we perceive something can influence how we think about money.

Sarah Newcomb is a behavioural economist who thinks that the traditional financial planning concept of thinking about cashflow and budgeting doesn't help people make good financial decisions.

In the cashflow model money is viewed like a river, flowing into and out of your life, to be directed by you, with hopefully some diverted into savings.

The problem as Newcomb sees it is that this thinking fails to identify the source of the income or the purpose of expenses, which makes them seem distant and out of a person's control.

Instead Newcomb suggests that it is better to think of money in terms of assets, not income, which in turn is derived from a resource.

So instead of thinking about your salary coming from your employer, it actually comes from you converting your own resources – time, energy and skills – that your employer leases from you.

'A simple shift of focus away from your employer and to your own role in generating your income could have a positive emotional benefit even if it doesn't change your situation. Second, by focusing on the source of income rather than the flow, you will be better equipped to make many types of beneficial financial decisions down the line.'[16]

This change of approach is more empowering and enables you to 'Focus on the spring, not the stream.'

This in turn enables you to protect and nurture the resources and assets that generate income.

Losing your job doesn't mean you've lost your skills, experience, contacts, reputation, time, energy or character.

In addition to generating income from labour, it can also come from land and capital.

Land can be farmed, rented, developed or mined.

Capital is anything that has financial value such as possessions (that can be sold for money), money (cash, shares, gold) and social capital (reputation, local amenities, bartering, sharing, personal contacts).

Newcomb defines assets and liabilities very simply.

A liability is something which costs more than it earns.

A house you live in, therefore, is a liability because you have to pay annual property tax, regular maintenance, heating and lighting, mortgage repayments and interest.

An asset is something that earns more than it costs.

The more you think in terms of money coming from your assets – human, financial, property, possessions – the more you'll be able to influence your income.

The more you understand the needs you're trying to meet through spending, the more you can influence where your income goes.

The more control you feel over your income and expenses, the greater sense of financial well-being you'll experience.

CONTROL OVER DAY-TO-DAY FINANCES

MANAGING YOUR MONEY, NOT YOUR MONEY MANAGING YOU

9

ZERO HERO

THE ONE THING YOU MUST DO EACH MONTH

*'Do not save what is left after spending;
instead spend what is left after saving'*

Warren Buffett, American business magnate,
investor, and philanthropist

Michelle McGagh is a financial journalist.

She and her husband earned a good income but they never seemed to have much in the way of savings, as money just seemed to disappear on things like cosmetics, nights out, taxis and takeaways.

Michelle didn't have credit cards and the only debt she and her husband had was the mortgage on their London home, into which they had recently moved.

As the house needed a fair bit of refurbishment they decided to put the bulk of their possessions into storage and made do with a few clothes, pots and pans and their bicycles.

Every few weeks Michelle found herself having to visit the storage unit to get something, and on one visit she found a box labelled 'Not needed'.

Michelle decided that she had to take some drastic action so she searched online 'Getting rid of stuff'.

After reading around the subject, she and her husband agreed that they would sell, give away or recycle as many of their possessions as they could.

Michelle explains 'I realised that the things I owned had started to "own" me, and I had bought things to tell people a story about who I was. By getting rid of those items I was taking back control of who I really was.'

They ended up getting rid of 80% of everything they owned.

Then Michelle found out about 'Buy nothing day' – a day when you buy absolutely nothing – which is fittingly held on the same day as the Black Friday shopping event.

She decided to see if she could 'buy nothing' for a whole year to see if it could force her to live a different life and make her happier.

Michelle started her no spend year on Black Friday, November 2015.

Other than paying her share of the mortgage, basic utility bills, insurance and a very small food and toiletries allowance, she stopped all spending.

No taxis, no drinks out, no takeaways, no foreign holidays, no beauty products, no clothes, no meals out.

Michelle and her husband cycled everywhere, including to a camping holiday in East Anglia.

When she met her friends in a bar she had a glass of tap water, and refused offers from her friends.

Being frugal made Michelle more creative, adventurous and flexible about her lifestyle.

She found lots of free activities like museums, galleries and open air concerts.

She volunteered at a music festival and got involved in an amateur dramatics group.

At the end of the year, by spending less, Michelle and her husband had saved nearly £23,000!

The first thing she bought was a round of drinks for her understanding and supportive group of close friends.

Then she used the £23,000 to reduce her mortgage because becoming debt-free as soon as possible is a very important priority for her.[17]

'When you give yourself a budget of zero, you don't give a s*** about spending any more,' explains Michelle.

'Not only is it a great feeling, not being beholden to a society that places consumerism and possession above all else, but also all that time I used to spend buying things I now have free to spend doing things I actually care about, things that enrich my life in a way that purchasing never ever could.'

Learning to use your money wisely and in line with what you say is important to you is essential to your financial well-being.

Have a good long look at a year's worth of your bank statements and work out where your money goes.

Then ask yourself if this spending making you happy and, if not, what would.

You have to weigh up whether the temporary happiness you derive from your short-term spending decisions is worth sacrificing longer term goals like becoming debt free, building up a sufficient emergency fund or saving for financial independence.

You don't have to get your spending to zero, but you do need to get it under control so you can live a life that reflects who you want to be, not what consumerism tells you to be.

And once you've done that you can make sure that the first bill that gets paid each month is the monthly savings or debt repayment amount for your future self.

10

BAD DAY AT THE OFFICE

WHEN YOU SHOULDN'T GO SHOPPING

'You can never have too many hats, gloves, and shoes.'

Patsy Stone – in British television comedy series
'Absolutely Fabulous'

A few years ago a chap who I know at my local gym – let's call him Doug – was hit for six when his wife announced that she wanted a divorce after twenty years of marriage.

Doug knew that their relationship wasn't brilliant but he didn't think it was that bad and he was concerned about the effect on their teenage daughter.

Over the next year Doug regularly updated me on the progress of his divorce, including the financial settlement negotiations.

Eventually Doug and his wife agreed the financial settlement, which included selling their home and sharing the proceeds.

One day Doug seemed quite down and I asked him what was wrong.

'I'm 54 years old!

'I don't have enough money to buy a house outright and I'm too old to get a mortgage to make up the difference, so I've got to rent and that will mean I can't save much towards my retirement,' said Doug.'

A few months later I saw Doug again and he seem a completely different man – happy and carefree.

'You look pleased with yourself,' I said.

'I am mate. Bought myself an amazing new car,' replied Doug.

'A new car! I thought you were trying to sort out somewhere to live?'

'I hit rock bottom and felt so down that I thought to myself f*** it! I'm going to treat myself.

'I saw advertised at a main dealer this amazing rare one year old supercar, with every possible extra fitted, that cost £120,000 new. I offered them £63,000 and they accepted,' he explained. 'I thought to myself things can't get any worse and if I can't enjoy myself now, when can I?'

What Doug didn't point out was the fact that the minimum cost of servicing his new car was £1,000 and the tyres were £300 each, so buying it was only the first expense.

Doug succumbed to what many people do when they suffer a setback or personal or professional disappointment – an urge to buy something expensive to assuage their bad feelings.

But apart from the obvious financial implications of impulsive, unnecessary spending, a recent study suggests that you might end up feeling even worse about yourself and even less able to resist future spending temptations.[18]

The study suggests that, instead of cheering you up, anything you buy that's associated with whatever you're trying to forget actually just serves to remind you of that setback or failure.

Instead of being a consolation prize it acts as a trigger that makes you feel even worse, chips away at your self-control and even impairs your ability to focus on completing difficult tasks.

'After experiencing a setback in one area of their life, consumers might be better off boosting their sense of self in a different area of their life,' the researchers say.

So when you've suffered a setback or disappointment try to cheer yourself up by doing something that doesn't involve spending much money.

11

I REALLY *NEED* IT!

GETTING A GRIP ON SPENDING

*'Anyone who lives within their means suffers
from a lack of imagination.'*

Oscar Wilde, Irish writer

Some years ago my wife went shopping with our youngest daughter Megan, who would have been about eight at the time.

They were browsing in a large department store looking for a birthday present for my wife's mother.

'Mummy, Mummy,' Megan called to my wife.

'I really, really need this necklace.' she said with wide eyes while holding up an inexpensive plastic bead necklace.

'Megan, you don't *need* that necklace, you *want* it and that's not the same,' replied my wife.

'No mummy I really *need* it.'.

'Why do you need it then?' asked my wife.

'Because it's pretty and I like pretty things,' Megan replied.

'No, *need* means you can't do without it because it's essential to your survival or well-being,' said my wife. '*Want* means it's not essential but you'd like it anyway because you think it is important and will make you happy.'

'Yes, yes, I really *want* it then because pretty things make me happy,' said Megan.

'Well Megan we've only got so much money to spend. We can either buy that necklace and not get granny a present or buy granny a present and leave the necklace. What do you want to do?' my wife asked.

Megan thought carefully for a moment.

"Well it wouldn't be nice not to give granny a present on her birthday, so we'll have to leave the necklace then," she said, deflated.

Like my wife, many people think that understanding the difference between wants and needs is the key to controlling spending.

Sarah Newcomb is a behavioural economist who disagrees with that thinking and thinks that all spending decisions are attempting to satisfy a need.

'We *know* we don't need a lot of the things that we buy. We want them because we believe they will help us meet some deeper need inside us. Even the frivolous items we buy on impulse are attempts to serve a fundamental need such as fun, comfort, ease, or relaxation. We need to learn the difference between a *need* and a *strategy*. This small change of wording creates a big change in perspective.'[19]

By accepting that all our needs are valid and need to be satisfied, we can then start to think about how we might meet that need without spending money, or at the very least spending less.

Newcomb explains that making a flask of coffee rather than visiting the local coffee shop doesn't meet the real need.

'By making coffee yourself, you eliminated the expense, but you didn't meet the real need. Maybe you're seeking human connection after hours of staring at a computer. Maybe you need a bit of relaxation, beauty, fun, or simply a change of pace to break up the monotony of the day. It could be that you have a need to connect with nature and the fresh air is what you are after. If you like to go with colleagues, you might be meeting a social need. Whatever it is, if you cut out an expense without devising a new strategy for meeting the need, you will find yourself unsatisfied.'[20]

So when thinking about your spending habits, start thinking what real needs you're trying to satisfy and what lower or no-cost strategies you might employ to meet them.

My daughter really did have a need all those years ago but, as she now knows, it didn't need £15 to be spent on a necklace to meet it!

12

MATTRESS MADNESS

WHY THERE IS NO SUCH THING AS A SALE

'Whoever said money can't buy happiness simply didn't know where to go shopping'

Bo Derek – American film actress

One day my wife advised me that we needed to buy a new mattress for our bed.

'Why do we need a new mattress?' I asked her.

'Because you should change your mattress every eight to ten years,' she replied.

'Who told you that?'

'I heard it on the radio in a bed shop advert.'

'Well they would say that, wouldn't they?'

'But we've had our mattress for 18 years, Jason, so we *must* replace it,' said my wife adamantly.

We duly trotted off to a bed shop.

As we entered the shop my wife exclaimed 'Look. This one is in a sale and has been reduced from £2,000 to £1,000.'

I looked carefully at the mattress and the 'special offer sale' sign.

'This isn't a special sale price, it's a mattress on sale for £1,000,' I said. 'The question is whether we like this £1,000 mattress or not. The fact that the shop is trying to make it look like a bargain, and trying to make us rush a decision before the 'offer' ends, is irrelevant.'

My wife looked at me doubtfully.

'Look, if you don't believe me I'll prove it to you,' I said.

I beckoned for the sales assistant, who had been hovering nearby, to come over.

'Could you please answer a question for me, and be totally honest?' I asked the assistant.

'Sure. What's your question?' she replied.

'How many of these mattresses have you personally sold at £2,000 in the past six months?' I asked.

The sales lady hesitated before replying 'Well… I've not personally sold any at that price.'

'How many of these have you sold at £1,000 over the same period?'

The sales lady looked pensively between me and my wife, 'Well I've sold quite a few of these at that price… £1,000.'

'So can we agree that the real price of this mattress is actually £1,000, and not £2,000, and this 'special offer' sign is just a marketing gimmick?' I asked.

'Well… I think that would be a fair assessment,' she replied.

I turned to my wife feeling vindicated.

She looked at me determinedly 'Well we still need to buy a mattress, so let's start trying out all these we can see and find some we like, and *then* compare prices.'

Unless a business is being liquidated and closed down, most sale promotions are merely designed to create a sense of urgency to get you to buy today and to give you some justification for making what is, almost always, an emotionally driven purchase.

So next time you are thinking about buying anything, but particularly more expensive products or services, forget any sale promotions and just focus on the net price being asked.

You can then compare net prices between different suppliers, and not against the supplier's own 'pre-sale' price.

13

CLUTTER-BUSTER

A SIMPLE WAY TO FEEL GOOD WITHOUT SPENDING

'Too often, a vast collection of possessions ends up possessing its owner. The asset I most value, aside from health, is interesting, diverse, and long-standing friends.'

Warren Buffett, American business magnate,
investor and philanthropist

My mum would describe her home as a bit disorganised.

I would describe it as cluttered, untidy, and full of useless rubbish.

My mum knows that I find her home environment extremely stressful and depressing but she seems happy with the way it is.

Some years ago, when we were speaking on the telephone my mum told me that she had recently had a thorough clear out.

'I hired some chaps to help me sort through everything and they've filled three mini-skips with stuff,' my mum proudly informed me.

'I've still got a little bit more to sort out but the bulk of the work is done,' she added.

A few weeks later I went to visit my mum.

As I walked through the front door into the hallway nothing looked any different.

The coat rack was still overflowing with an array of garments, three vacuum cleaners were stacked in the corner, there were soft toys perched on the lower steps of the stairs and a new lampshade on the floor, still wrapped in its packaging.

The sitting room didn't seem any different either.

There was stuff everywhere.

'I thought you filled up three mini-skips with stuff, mum?' I said.

'I did,' she replied.

'What, with everyone else's junk except your own?'

My eye was then caught by a two-foot high Father Christmas sitting on top of a large square base.

'Well, why have you still got this useless thing?' I asked, nodding towards Father Christmas.

'That's not rubbish, I've only just bought it,' my mum replied defiantly.

'But it's May. Why do you want a Father Christmas statue in the summer?'

'I like to plan ahead, and anyway it's not a statue. It dances when you clap your hands. Look,' Mum said, and with that she clapped her hands.

Father Christmas started to sing 'Rockin' Around the Christmas Tree' while doing a strange sort of dancing movement.

My mum thought it was hilarious and was laughing and despite myself I found myself also laughing out loud.

I spent the rest of my visit trying to help my mum get a bit more organised and get rid of more rubbish but it was a slow process.

Despite my best efforts my mum will always live in a muddle but if that makes her happy then I just have to accept it.

But there is a lot of evidence that regular decluttering of your home contributes to overall well-being and happiness and also helps reduce impulsive spending on new possessions.

Some estimates suggest that the typical home has £3,500 worth of unused items, so getting rid of unwanted items can also improve your bank balance.

Kerri Richardson is the author of 'What Your Clutter is Trying to Tell You' and she has devised a simple approach that helps people get rid of 465 things from their home in a month.[21]

Kerri explains:

"Starting [on the 1st of the month], and for each day your challenge is to get rid of the number of items that corresponds to the date.

Here's how it goes:

1st: Choose one item to get rid of

2nd: Choose two items to get rid of

3rd: Choose three items to get rid of

And so on.

It's like a treasure hunt! And by the end of the 30-day month, **you will have cleared 465 items!**

Sending items to landfill should be the last resort.

Send shoes and clothes to a clothes bank or charity shop.

Give half-used cans of paint to local artists.

Sell anything that you can on Ebay or Gumtree – you'll be amazed what people will buy.

Give other useable items to charity shops.

Take everything that can be recycled to the local recycling centre.

You may occasionally come across an item which you have forgotten about and really want to keep and that's OK.

But you'll need to find another item to get rid of in its place.

Whenever I buy a new possession or item of clothing I find an existing item to get rid of.

Decluttering isn't a panacea but it should help you avoid buying things you don't need, help you turn unused items into cash and create a greater sense of control and order in your life.

One thing is for sure though.

I won't be buying a singing Father Christmas anytime soon.

14

CARD CANCER

'Never spend your money before you have it.'

Thomas Jefferson,
Former President of the United States

I grew up in the 1970s and early 1980s.

Neither of my parents earned high salaries. As a result we never had much money and our lifestyle was extremely modest.

My parents separated when I was about six. Me and my two older brothers continued living with our mum in our tiny rented terraced house in South East London.

My dad made a financial contribution each month but it was always a struggle for my mum to make ends meet. Back then mum wasn't the type of person who would dream of applying for benefits so she did three jobs to make ends meet.

About this time my mum's bank wrote to her offering a credit card.

Credit cards were a relatively new thing at that time but more and more shops accepted them for payment on goods and services.

My mum duly signed up for a credit card.

When my mum first received the credit card she was excited and eager to go shopping. The credit card offered her the possibility to buy things she wouldn't ordinarily be able to. Mum went from shop to shop buying shoes, dresses, a hat, and she even bought a new television!

On that shopping trip my mum went from being someone who had nothing to someone who could have almost anything.

I remember getting home with her and the excitement of going through the bags and looking at all the things we bought.

Over the next few weeks it was like we had won the lottery. New things appeared almost every day.

Mum was happier than I'd seen her for many years.

But very abruptly the new things stopped arriving. Mum started getting very irritable and snappy.

Then one day I heard my older brother, who was wise beyond his 13 years, say to my mum 'But this is borrowing, it's not free money, mum!'

My brother, who is a genius at maths, then explained to my mum how much interest she'd pay each month on all the items she'd bought on her credit card and how long it would take her to repay the debt.

My mum looked crestfallen and defeated.

'I just wanted to buy some nice things, that's all,' she said.

'Mum, you can't buy what you can't afford, and if you do you'll forever be paying high interest and monthly repayments.'

In the UK today the typical household has an outstanding credit card debt of about £2,500, which, at the average minimum payment and with interest added, would take just over 26 years to repay.[22]

Credit cards, store cards, overdrafts and most bank loans are what we call **bad debt** because they are mainly used to enable people to spend more than they earn or have saved and charge double-digit interest rates for the privilege.

Credit cards do offer a secure way of buying goods and services (and in the UK give protection against faulty goods or services) but they are also an easy way to fall into uncontrollable debt.

Research also shows that paying by debit or credit card increases both impulsive spending[23] and the amount[24] we are prepared to pay for something compared to using physical cash.

My advice is to avoid credit cards and instead use cash to buy smaller items and a debit card to pay for more expensive transactions but only with money you already have.

If you really must have a credit card have just ONE with a relatively LOW credit limit and make sure that you only spend on the card what you have budgeted for and ensure that the balance is repaid each month.

Avoid any cards which reward you for spending, because you don't want to give yourself an excuse to spend more than you need.

Someone once said to me that the best way to give up cigarettes – and minimise the chance of getting cancer – is never to start smoking.

The best way to avoid *bad* debt is never to accrue it in the first place, by only spending what you have on what you really need.

15

ON YOUR BIKE

A RETHINK ON CAR OWNERSHIP

'If you think nobody cares if you're alive,
try missing a couple of car payments.'

Earl Wilson, American journalist,
gossip columnist and author

I got my first car when I was seventeen.

It was a dull grey Vauxhall Viva with black plastic seats.

In today's terms it cost me about £500 and the annual insurance cost about £350.

It had no radio and a temperamental heater that made the car smell of curry. It drank almost as much oil as fuel.

But the feature that caused me the most trouble was the erratic starter motor.

When it refused to work I had to either whack it with a hammer or bump-start the engine.

If I couldn't park on a hill, which was often the case, and the hammer didn't wake up the starter motor, I could only bump start the car if I had a passenger or could corral a passer-by to help push it.

My girlfriend at the time was none too pleased if we were going out for the evening, and she had to start pushing the car in her high heels (she didn't drive, so I couldn't do the pushing).

Thirty years later my current car is a lot more comfortable (and reliable) than that old Vauxhall, but it is also a lot more expensive.

The cost of car insurance for young people has skyrocketed over the past decade, to the extent that is can be almost as much as the value of the vehicle. This often makes it unaffordable without financial help from their family.

The advent of ride hailing apps like Uber and Lyft, and the eventual availability of autonomous electric cars, together with wider adoption of car-sharing and better public transport, as well as rising vehicle running costs, are combining to undermine car ownership among younger people in urban areas.

'Our intention is to make Uber so efficient, cars so highly utilized, that for most people it is cheaper than owning a car.' said Uber's then CEO Travis Kalanick in 2015.

Interestingly the majority of UK automotive executives expect that more than half of today's car owners will not want to own a car in less than a decade.[25]

While car ownership may always be relevant for families and those living in more remote rural places, it looks like young single urban dwellers will increasingly turn to alternative mobility as a service (MaaS) model.

But if you do want or need to own a car, there is a better way to do so then taking out expensive and inflexible car finance.

Pete Matthews is a UK-based financial adviser who also runs a personal finance education website called Meaningful Money.

Pete gives an example of someone buying a £20,000 car with a £2,000 deposit and car finance of £18,000 over 5 years with payments of £400 per month.

In this scenario the total cost of the car amounts to £26,000 (£2,000 + (60 x £400).

The car will also depreciate by £15,000 over the period, so ends up being worth £5,000.

Paying £26,000 for something that ends up being worth £5,000 isn't a good deal.

Pete suggests that, if you can change your mindset and accept not driving the 'coolest' car initially, you can end up with a very nice car at a much lower cost than by using the traditional car finance approach.

Here's how you can achieve that with the same £2,000 deposit and £400 per month budget.

In year one you buy a £2,000 car and save £400 per month into an instant-access savings account.

In the second and subsequent years you sell the car and use the proceeds, together with the balance of the monthly savings account, to fund a more expensive car as set out in the table opposite.

Year	1	2	3	4	5
Car value start	£2,000	£6,300	£10,300	£13,800	£16,800
Car value end	£1,500	£5,500	£9,000	£12,000	£15,000
Amount saved (12 x £400)	£4,800	£4,800	£4,800	£4,800	£4,800
Car proceeds	£6,300	£10,300	£13,800	£16,800	£19,800

Source: www.meaningfulmoney.tv

In the example shown in the table, after five years you'd have a car worth nearly £20,000 and be better off by £14,800 (the difference between a cost of £6,200 and a cost of £21,000).*

So think carefully: does it make sense to own a car or would it be better to walk, cycle, use public transport, taxis, ride-hail, or occasionally rent a vehicle?

If you still think you do need to own a car then think about adopting Pete Matthew's alternative funding approach.

It might take you a bit longer but eventually you'll end up with a cool set of wheels, just at a fraction of the cost.

---

* The cost of the traditional approach would be £21,000 because £26,000 has been outlaid compared to the vehicle final value of £5,000. The cost of the alternative approach would be £6,200 because £26,000 has been outlaid compared to the final vehicle value of £19,800.

CAPACITY TO ABSORB A FINANCIAL SHOCK

BEING ABLE TO COPE WITH THE FINANCIAL CHALLENGES OF UNFORESEEN LIFE EVENTS

16

IT NEVER RAINS, IT POURS!

THE KEY THING YOU NEED IN CASE OF A FINANCIAL EMERGENCY

*'I'm the only person I know that's lost a
quarter of a billion dollars in one year....
It's very character-building.'*

Steve Jobs, American entrepreneur, businessman,
inventor and industrial designer

Many years ago I had a client, let's call him Gary, who ran a reasonably large public relations company.

Gary owned a big house in North London.

He owned several rental properties.

He had three cars – a brand new Bentley, an Aston Martin and a Range Rover.

Gary was married to Lisa, who was well-educated, articulate and immaculately dressed.

They had two children. Both went to expensive private schools in London.

The family went on exotic holidays all around the world, they threw lavish parties and generally enjoyed life to the full.

Gary was lots of fun and very good company, but...

Gary would never heed my advice to try to control his spending and build up some sensible cash reserves in both his business and personal life.

One evening Gary and Lisa were on their way to an exclusive black tie charity ball being held in an upmarket hotel in Central London.

Gary looked dashing in his tuxedo and bow tie and Lisa looked amazing in an expensive ball gown.

They drove to the hotel in their new Bentley.

'I just need to stop at the cash machine and get out some money for the raffle,' said Gary.

Gary stopped at a cash machine and inserted his card.

The machine informed Gary that he had no available funds and spat out his card.

'I can't get any cash out. What are we going to do, Lisa?' he said.

'Let's pop by at my friend Claire's and borrow some cash from her. She's on the way,' replied Lisa.

And with that they sped over to Claire's home.

Claire was Lisa's best friend, who was at that time training to be a nurse and living in a tiny student nurse flat attached to a major London teaching hospital.

Student nurses don't earn very much money.

'Hi Claire, we're in a bit of bind. Can we borrow £250 off you as we can't get any cash out of the machine?' asked Lisa.

'Sure, if you can you drive me to the cash machine,' replied Claire.

And with that they all sped off to the nearest ATM.

Gary and Lisa went to the ball, gave generously to the raffle and repaid Claire her money.

Gary and Lisa's life eventually fell apart because of their failure to build a cash reserve for various financial shocks they underwent, most notably a big drop in Gary's income when his firm went bust.

One of the biggest causes of homelessness and accumulation of 'bad' debt is unexpected expenses (like home or car repairs) or loss of income due to illness, disability or redundancy.

Being able to cope with financial shocks is the foundation of financial well-being.

The first element of that foundation is to build up a sufficient cash reserve that can be used in the event of an emergency.

If you have accumulated any 'bad' debt, make sure that you stop adding to it and then focus on getting rid of it.

But as soon as you have got rid of the 'bad' debt, focus on building up your cash reserve.

The old rule of thumb I was taught was to have at least six months' worth of expenditure in a cash reserve, adjusted up or down depending on the situation and preferences.

For example, if you are wholly reliant on your income from working, and your employer doesn't offer more than basic state disability benefits, you'd probably want to hold nearer to six months' expenses.

However, if you have passive income (dividends, rental, royalties etc.) and a partner who also works, then you might feel fine holding just two or three months' worth of expenses.

But there is now a more robust and effective way to calculate and work towards building an adequate emergency cash reserve.

HelloWallet is an independent, online and mobile financial wellness software application provided by US companies that employ over 2.5 million workers.

By analysing the anonymous banking transactions of users, HelloWallet has developed a methodology for determining a more personalised emergency savings target for most workers.[26]

Emergency expenses are categorised as either minor, major or job loss related as shown in table 1.

TABLE 1: TYPES OF EMERGENCY RECOMMENDATIONS AND HOW HELLOWALLET CALCULATE THEM

TYPE OF EMERGENCY	
Minor emergency	Minor Car Repair + Minor Home Repair + Healthcare Deductible
Major emergency	Maximum of: Major Car Repair; Major Home Repair; Out-of-pocket Healthcare Costs
Job loss	1 Year of Expenses – Secondary Income for Year – Unemployment Benefits/passive income

Source: HelloWallet

Minor expenses are the most common but tend to be fleeting and have less impact and the researchers recommend people start saving for these expenses to build confidence and self-discipline

The average suggested amounts, based on US data, are shown in table 2.

TABLE 2: EXAMPLE OF MINOR EMERGENCY FUND RECOMMENDATION CALCULATION

Type of Emergency	Individual Who Doesn't Own Home or Car	Individual With Car	Family With Car and Home
Car	$0	$750	$750
Home	$0	$0	$1,800
Health	$1,300	$1,300	$2,600
Grand total	$1,300	$2,050	$5,150

Source: HelloWallet

Major expenses are less common but can have a big impact on family finances.

HelloWallet's suggested calculations for major expenses is shown in table 3.

TABLE 3: EXAMPLE OF MAJOR EMERGENCY FUND RECOMMENDATION CALCULATION

Type of Emergency	Individual Who Doesn't Own Home or Car	Individual With Car	Family With Car and Home
Car	$0	$3,800	$3,800
Home	$0	$0	$10,000
Health	$2,500	$2,500	$5,000
Grand total	$2,500	$3,800	$10,000

Source: HelloWallet

Losing income from employment due to illness, disability or redundancy can have the most severe impact on your financial position, and requires the highest amount of emergency savings.

For example, if Simon and Chloe have monthly expenses of $4,000 and take-home incomes of $1,500 and $3,000 respectively, they would need $22,000 in emergency savings to protect themselves from Chloe losing her job for 12 months.

In total, they would need $48,000 to cover their expenses, and Simon could be expected to bring in $18,000 from his job, while rental income from a second home would provide another $7,800.

TABLE 4: STEPS TO CALCULATE EMERGENCY RECOMMENDATIONS AND EXAMPLE

Consideration	Calculation	Total for Prototypical Couple
Replace expenses for one year	Expenses x 12	$48,000
Reduce by: Second income Rental income	Net income x 12 Net income x 12	$18,000 $7,800
		$22,200

Source: HelloWallet

However, you calculate it, once you have accumulated an adequate cash reserve you'll not only be more financially resilient, you'll feel more secure and in control, which will increase your financial well-being.

The key is to fix the roof when the sun is shining, not when it is pouring with rain!

17

HIGH-WIRE ACT

WHY IT MAKES SENSE TO HAVE
A SAFETY NET

'You miss 100% of the shots you don't take.'

Wayne Gretzky,
Canadian former professional ice-hockey player

My brother-in-law has a very eclectic and bohemian group of friends.

'Mad' Mikey was one such friend. He got his nickname because he looked like something out of a Mad Max movie – shaven head, piercings and tattoos everywhere and an enormous motorbike.

Mikey lived with his long-term partner and their two young children in a small rented rural home and he held down a job as a building site foreman.

Mikey's lifestyle was simple and modest, but he seemed happy and he was great fun.

One day on his way home from work on his motorbike, Mikey overtook a tractor and was hit head-on by an oncoming truck. He was killed instantly.

Thankfully Mikey had had the foresight and wherewithal to take out a life insurance policy for a sizeable amount several years earlier.

Had 'Mad' Mikey not have taken out that policy, his partner would not only have had to cope with the emotional loss, but also the significant financial loss arising from his death.

The insurance money gave her choices, such as how much she would choose to work and where she wanted to live.

Research shows that spending on the right type and level of insurance helps improve our overall financial well-being, as it helps us feel more in control, which is in itself an essential element of life satisfaction and happiness.[27]

In order of importance you need to buy enough insurance to cover the following personal risks:

- **Income replacement insurance** – If you are still working and reliant on your income to fund your lifestyle then this insurance will pay a proportion of your income if you are unable to work due to illness or disability. It starts after a waiting period and continues until you recover or get to the nominated retirement age.

- **Life insurance** – If you have dependants then they'll need a lump sum to repay any debts and fund ongoing lifestyle costs in the event of your death. If you don't have any or sufficient cover through your job, then a *lump sum term policy* is the cheapest and simplest type of cover. You can also buy cover which pays out a specific monthly or yearly amount for the balance of the policy term, known as *family income benefit*, which can be cheaper and simpler than a lump sum policy.

- **Critical illness insurance** – If you have loans or other obligations that you'd want to be able to repay in the event that you became permanently disabled or suffered a serious illness like cancer or a stroke, then this insurance will pay a lump sum on diagnosis. It's quite expensive, though, so you might view it as a nice to have rather than an essential.

- **Health insurance** – Depending on the quality of your local health service you might want to be able to fund private health insurance, to ensure you get access to medical treatment. This cover gets more expensive with age but costs can be kept low by having a high claims excess.

Someone told me many years ago: 'Insure for what can go wrong, so you can invest for what can go right'.

Delegating the financial risk of death, illness or disability to an insurance company might not be exciting or glamorous, but it is a smart move.

18

DOWN BUT NOT OUT

HOW TO AVOID CAUSING HEARTACHE AND ANGUISH

'Life is hard, after all, it kills you.'

Katherine Hepburn, American actress

After a long career in the British Army, including serving in the Gulf war, Paul Briggs joined Merseyside Police in 2004.

In 2007 Paul became a motorcycle traffic officer, a job he loved.

Paul and his wife Lindsey, whom he'd met when she was a teenager, had been married for fifteen years and they had a four year old daughter, Ella.

At about 8pm on 3rd July 2015 Paul, who was 42, waved goodbye to his wife and daughter and drove off to start a night shift in Liverpool.

As he approached a left-hand bend, Paul swerved to avoid colliding with a Nissan Micra, which was being driven on the wrong side of the road.

Paul hit the oncoming car and was thrown from his motorbike.

Despite wearing a helmet, Paul suffered serious brain damage and as a result lay unresponsive in his hospital bed.

After about a year, when it became clear that Paul's condition had not changed, and there seemed little prospect of any improvement, Lindsey asked the doctors to withdraw treatment from Paul to enable him to die.

According to Lindsey and other members of Paul's family, he had previously commented on the case of Michael Schumacher, who was left in a coma after a skiing accident and he had said he 'would not want to live like that'.

But Paul's doctors said it would be wrong to withdraw treatment as he was in a 'minimally conscious state' but not a 'permanent vegetative state'.

They also said Paul would benefit from being moved to a specialist rehabilitation centre and 'a more socially stimulating environment'.

Lindsey and Paul's family had to commence legal proceedings against the health trust that was treating Paul, to compel Paul's doctors to remove the artificial feeding and hydration that was keeping him alive.

Over the next six months Lindsey and her lawyers had several hearings with the Court of Protection, which looks after and determines cases that involve people who lack mental capacity to make decisions for themselves.

Finally, in December 2016, the judge agreed with Lindsey and Paul's family that Paul should be allowed to die, and instructed doctors to withdraw feeding and hydration.

Lawyers acting for the hospital trust advised that they might fight the ruling and take the case to a higher court, thereby prolonging the stress and emotional strain for Lindsey and Paul's family.

Thankfully the hospital decided not to contest the decision and Paul eventually died on 22nd January 2017.

Lindsey and Paul's family could have been spared much of the emotional stress involved in taking the hospital to court if he had created what is commonly known as a 'living will' or 'advanced medical directive'.

This is a legal document in which a person specifies what actions should be taken for their health if they are no longer able to make decisions for themselves because of illness or incapacity.

In England and Wales this document is known as a **Health & Welfare Lasting Power of Attorney** (LPA) whereas in the USA it is known as an **advance healthcare directive**.*

You can also arrange an LPA (or equivalent for your country) to enable nominated people to make financial decisions for you if you lose the ability to do so yourself.

In the UK the document can be created for free online, although there is typically a small fee (between £75-82 at time of writing) to register the document to make it valid.

Clearly older people are more likely to suffer mental incapacity, but, as the case of Paul Briggs shows, this can and does affect younger people.

Statistics from Stroke Association in the UK shows that about 25% of strokes are suffered by those under age 65. Men are at a 25% higher risk and tend to have them at a younger age than women.[28]

---

* Most countries and jurisdictions have some form of legally-recognised living will, although their names and legal powers vary.

Choosing who you want to make important decisions about your medical treatment or financial affairs if you are not mentally capable, and ensuring your wishes and preferences are legally recorded, will avoid a lot of heartache and anguish for your family.

19

THE BIG DIPPER

HOW TO TAME THE STOCKMARKET

'October: This is one of the particularly dangerous months to invest in stocks. Other dangerous months are July, January, September, April, November, May, March, June, December, August and February.'

Mark Twain, American writer, humourist, entrepreneur, publisher, and lecturer

Nigel was in his late forties, highly educated, articulate, and a very experienced businessman who had been a client of my firm for about five years.

He had recently stepped down as the CEO of a very large business and had since taken on a number of non-executive directorships.

In early 2009, in the midst of the global financial crisis, Nigel had arranged a meeting with me to discuss the investment portfolio that we had built and continued to monitor for him.

'I want to encash my portfolio and move to cash until things settle down a bit,' Nigel told me.

'I see,' I replied thoughtfully.

'I really think things are going to get even worse,' he continued.

'Right,' I responded.

'Look, markets have fallen about 50% in the past eighteen months, so now I need to get 100% return on my money just to get back to the previous value.'

I sat looking at Nigel, saying nothing.

'I can see markets falling by another 50%, I really can,' he said.

I replied 'Nigel, do you still have faith in the future of capitalism?'

'Well, overall yes, notwithstanding the current turbulence,' he replied.

'Do you really think people will want to give up their nice lifestyles, all their luxuries, all their electronic gadgets, their foreign holidays, their social life, their hobbies, their sport?' I asked him.

'No, I don't think they will' he said.

'Do you remember we set out your goals, your resources, a projection of your short-term cashflow and of your lifetime liquid wealth?'

'Yes. You and your team helped to create it and update it each year,' Nigel replied.

'Have you got enough cash on hand to pay for emergencies or one off spending?' I asked.

'Yes, I do.'

'In fact, your cash reserve is three times more than you said you needed when we created the original plan, because I suggested it,' I replied.'

'And Nigel, is it still the case that your investment portfolio is intended to be used to meet your personal needs when you reach your mid 70s and leave a decent-sized legacy to a range of charities when you eventually die?'

'Yes.'

I sat quietly.

Nigel thought for a moment.

'I'm being irrational aren't I?'.

I said nothing.

'I'm letting my emotions get in the way and cause me to do something silly aren't I?' he said.

After a few moments of silence I said to Nigel 'It's perfectly understandable that you feel uncomfortable with the current economic situation.

'It's OK to feel anxious when you've seen your investment portfolio fall in value in a short space of time. It's also OK to question whether you need to make any changes to your plan in the light of these events.

'Now, I will certainly proceed with your instruction to sell your portfolio's holdings and move it all to cash if that is what you really, really want.

'But part of my job is to stop you doing silly things that will destroy your wealth, and selling your long-term portfolio when markets have fallen 50% in eighteen months, when you don't need the money now, is a very silly thing to do.'

Nigel sat and thought for a minute and then said 'I know in my head that you're right and I appreciate you questioning me, because nothing in my personal situation has changed and I can afford to sit this out for a few decades or more if necessary.'

After a few moments Nigel said 'Let's leave it all as it is.'

Stockmarkets have been described as voting machines in the short term, reflecting investors' current sentiments and supply and demand, and weighing machines in the long-term, reflecting the true value of companies.

Investing in companies is to own a part of their current and future profits.

Companies make profits if they sell products and services that people are willing and able to buy.

Sometimes companies do this well and make good profits and sometimes they do this badly and make poor profits or even losses.

Sometimes a company can be well run but the wider economy can be experiencing difficulties, when money is tight and people spend less.

As we saw in the global financial crisis, shocks to the global financial system can see the value of investment markets fall rapidly and sharply.

As a general rule stockmarkets are falling one third of the time, recovering one third of the time, and rising another third of the time.

Sometimes, as in the case of the Japanese stockmarket (the capital value of which at the time of writing is a little over 50% of its 1989 peak), the fall in value can last for decades.

So because the return from equities (part ownership in businesses) vary so much, that makes them one of the most risky type of investments.

This risk, in the form of a wide range of potential return outcomes, is actually the source of their higher expected return over the long-term compared to cash deposits and fixed income securities.

You therefore need to get used to seeing your capital fall in value on a regular basis if you want to earn a higher return.

But this is easier said than done, mainly because people prefer avoiding losses to acquiring gains – a phenomenon known as loss *aversion*.[29]

Research shows that people give twice the weight to the pain of loss than they do the pleasure of gain.

This means we seek risk when pursuing gains but become risk adverse in relation to losses, and are more likely to act if threatened with loss than promised gain.

As long as you have a big enough cash reserve, a long enough time horizon and have a good spread of global companies, all you need to control is your emotions when investment markets take a tumble.

The key to having a successful investment experience is to focus on the bigger picture, don't pay too much attention to the daily movements of your investments and let go of the past. You can't do anything about that.

20

PASSING THE BATON

WHY NOMINATING BENEFICIARIES IS ESSENTIAL

'Success depends upon previous preparation, and without such preparation there is sure to be failure.'

Confucius, Chinese teacher, editor, politician, and philosopher

Michael was at the top of his game as main board director of a very large international bank based in London.

Highly intelligent, urbane, cultured and well-read, he enjoyed life and all that it had to offer.

In his mid 50s, Michael had never married and lived on his own in a large penthouse overlooking the River Thames.

But despite his status and wealth, Michael made time to help people less fortunate than him, including helping at homeless drop-in centres and mentoring people with mental health and addiction problems.

If was through his charitable work that Michael came to know Emily.

Emily had grown up in an abusive and neglectful home, followed by a succession of foster carers and finally a children's home.

Emily then drifted into petty crime, drug addiction and prostitution.

By the time Michael met Emily when she was 28 she had three children and was undergoing treatment to help her stay off drugs and avoid her children being taken into care.

Michael developed a warm and fatherly type relationship with Emily, and he supported her in her efforts to rebuild her life.

Slowly but surely, with Michael's help, Emily gradually turned her life around.

A few years after first meeting Emily, Michael learned that he had a terminal illness which meant he would be unlikely to live more than a year.

Emily was very upset to think she would lose the only real friend she had ever known and feared that she might slip back into her old life.

Michael sat Emily down and explained that his sizeable pension benefits would be lost once he died as he had no spouse or financial dependants.

He therefore suggested that if he and Emily were to get married, she would be entitled to a widow's pension after his death, and thus provide her with a significant and secure income for the rest of her life.

In addition, Michael would leave his property in trust to Emily to use in her lifetime, whereupon it would pass to several charities which helped homeless and mentally ill people.

So, a month later, Michael and Emily were legally married.

Michael died about eight months later.

Emily then started to receive a monthly pension income of about £7,000 per month, a tax-free lump sum of £350,000 and the right to live in Michael's apartment.

Emily and her family have gone from strength to strength on the basis of the financial security which Michael's pension benefits have provided.

Few people will have to take the drastic step of marrying someone to avoid the loss of their pension benefits on their eventual demise.

But everyone with pension benefits and employer-provided life insurance should ensure that they advise their scheme's trustees of who they want to benefit from their pension benefits in the event of their death.

This is done by completing what is known as a 'nomination of beneficiaries' declaration.

In most countries the trustees have ultimate discretion over how they distribute any death lump sums but they will usually follow the deceased's wishes.

In the UK this also means that all payments withdrawn by beneficiaries from a non-defined benefits pension will be tax-free if the scheme member dies before age 75.

So make sure you complete and keep up to date your pension death benefits nomination to avoid causing those you leave behind even more heartache and anguish.

FINANCIAL FREEDOM TO MAKE CHOICES TO ENJOY LIFE

BEING ABLE TO AFFORD NEEDS, WANTS AND TO BE GENEROUS TOWARDS OTHERS

21

FLOWER POWER

WHY YOUR CAREER CHOICE IS SO
IMPORTANT TO HAPPINESS

'All my life, I always wanted to be somebody.
Now I see that I should have been more specific.'

Jane Wagner, American writer, director and producer

I was a financial planner for 25 years, and for seventeen of these I was running the firm I founded.

Despite the ups and downs, on balance I enjoyed my work and it certainly gave me a good income and nice lifestyle.

I loved the intellectual stimulation, I met many interesting people and I was well-respected and highly trusted.

There was just one problem – after a while I found my work didn't make me really happy and fulfilled.

A financial services business is subject to regulation and there are lots of principles, rules, processes and procedures to follow. The nature of the work means that accuracy, precision and attention to detail are prerequisites, and these pervade every person and part of the business.

Then one day I took a personality assessment.

It suggested that my work should allow me to be creative, give me high levels of autonomy and control, provide lots of variety, and enable me to improvise.

Although I was more than capable of following processes and doing detailed work, it clearly wasn't my natural mode of working; over many years I had learnt to adapt my behaviour to the needs of the business.

A few years ago the opportunity arose for me to sell my share of the business to the other shareholders.

I didn't have a big master plan for my life outside of the business, but I knew I wanted to focus on writing, speaking and being entrepreneurial.

I've now created a great lifestyle where each day is different and I only do the work and projects that I want.

I read, research, write, give talks and consult to businesses.

I've invested in a number of financial technology start-ups.

I have plenty of time to think, exercise and eat healthily.

I'm now far, far happier and satisfied with my life.

Research based on global data found that the happiest people tend to have a very high job fit and work between 35-44 hours a week.[30]

Another study found a big gap in life satisfaction between those who were employed and self-employed, with the self-employed having the highest life satisfaction.[31]

Research in the UK found that 87% of florists and gardeners said they were happy, compared to only 48% of IT workers and 44% of bankers.[32]

The evidence and my own experience suggests you'll probably be happiest if you choose a job that best fits your personality and innate skills, rather than that which pays you the most money.

Working with your hands (particularly connected with nature) and being self-employed, both which positively affect happiness, are optional extras!

22

THE STRAIGHTJACKET

WHY BEING AN EMPLOYEE MIGHT NOT BE RIGHT FOR YOU

'The biggest risk is not taking any risk. In a world that is changing really quickly, the only strategy that is guaranteed to fail is not taking risks.'

Mark Zuckerberg, American computer programmer and Internet entrepreneur

My first full-time job, at seventeen, was working for a company in London which stored the master copies of geological survey maps for all the big oil companies.

Most of the facility was in a basement and my job was to be locked in the windowless map vault and deal with the daily requests to retrieve and file the original maps.

The work was mind-numbingly boring and I only got to see anyone else at lunchtime, and I couldn't even get a signal to listen to the radio!

My salary was about £10,000 per annum in today's money, which wasn't bad for someone with no qualifications, no experience or real living costs.

Over the next few years I had several different jobs, including a stint as a civil servant.

The civil service back then was a very hierarchical organisation with a rigid grade structure.

It didn't seem to me that people got promoted or paid based on their ability or contribution, but how long they had been there, whether there was a vacancy and whether the interview went well.

I eventually came to the conclusion that I wasn't going to be able to enjoy life and build wealth working as an employee for the civil service or any other organisation.

Completely by chance I ended up as a self-employed life insurance salesman when I was 21.

If I didn't sell policies, I didn't get paid.

For many people this might have seemed scary but at the time I saw it as an opportunity to increase my earnings.

It was hard at the beginning to learn the products, processes and procedures.

But eventually I got quite good at selling and I started to earn a good living.

By the time I was 25 I was earning the equivalent of about £80,000 a year in today's prices.

After a few years I moved to a firm that had a wider product range and started dealing with better-off customers and increased my earnings.

By the time I was 29 I had acquired advanced professional qualifications and a lot of experience and felt that I was ready to start my own firm.

The first five years were extremely difficult. I made just about every mistake there is to make and I almost went bust.

Slowly but surely the business became successful and I built a small team of brilliant people and a loyal client base.

At age 46 I sold my stake to the other shareholders for a substantial amount and left the business. I wanted to focus on speaking and writing about financial well-being and also to invest in financial technology businesses.

Had I stayed an employee when I was young, working for someone, I doubt I'd ever have built sufficient wealth to be able to live the life I have now.

Being an entrepreneur and running a business isn't right for everyone but you owe it to your future self to at least consider it.

23
ONLY THE BEST

HOW WHAT WE PAY CAN INFLUENCE HAPPINESS

'In victory, you deserve Champagne. In defeat you need it.'

Napoleon Bonaparte, French military leader

I regularly have dinner with three of my friends, and the main focus of the evening isn't the food but drinking wine and having a good chat.

One of my friends is a real wine expert and his collection is worth a lot of money.

For the past few years my wine friend has been bringing a bottle from his collection so we can compare and contrast this to something from the restaurant's wine list.

On a recent night out we ordered from the wine list what my friend described as 'a pleasant but unremarkable red'.

Despite being 'unremarkable' this bottle of wine still cost £60!

At the same time my friend asked the restaurant to uncork a bottle which he had brought with him from his personal collection.

He went on to explain that he had paid about £50 for this bottle some years ago, but because it was so special the current open market value had risen to about £300.

Luckily we only had to share the cost of what my friend paid for it, not the current value.

The two wines were duly decanted and brought to the table to 'breathe' while we had an aperitif.

Both wines were then poured into separate glasses for each of us.

My friend went on to explain the differences in the wines, the smell, the colour and finally the taste.

As my friend was speaking he was clearly emotionally engaged with his 'special' wine but was diffident towards the restaurant wine.

The wine my friend had brought certainly tasted very nice but it didn't taste five times nicer than the restaurant-supplied wine.

In fact the week before my wife and I had shared a bottle of very inexpensive wine which we had bought from a discount supermarket for about £6 and I enjoyed that just as much as my friend's expensive wine.

So why is it that people are prepared to pay so much for some wines?

Well it certainly isn't the taste.

Lots of research has proven that most people can't really tell the difference between cheap and expensive wines when they taste blind (without knowing what they are drinking), and even tend to rate cheaper wines more highly.[33]

In fact it has been proven that we gain more pleasure from drinking a wine that we have been told is expensive, and less pleasure from one we have been told is cheap, even when the wines are exactly the same.[34]

But new research now explains why we get more pleasure from drinking expensive wines.[35]

It appears that our expectations influence how we think, feel and respond to a given situation.

So if we think an expensive wine is going to be a highly pleasurable and special experience, the pleasure we get from drinking it increases.

The research suggests that people do vary in terms of how susceptible they are to marketing effects like price and perceptions of quality, and this is particularly strong among people who seek instant rewards and pleasures (known as a high reward-seeking propensity).

Spending a lot of money on fine wines might give you slightly more pleasure than if you drank cheaper bottles, but they won't necessarily taste better.

Unless you are really passionate about wine and enjoy researching and collecting it as a hobby, buying cheaper wine is a better use of your hard-earned money and will still bring you pleasure.

So next time you want a bottle of wine just choose a cheap one and tell yourself it's really, really expensive.

24

THE BEATEN-UP PIANO

HOW TO GET MAXIMUM HAPPINESS FROM BUYING POSSESSIONS

'Whoever wants to reach a distant goal must take small steps'

Saul Bellow, Canadian-American writer

When I was a young child I really wanted to learn to play the piano.

By the time I was thirteen I had managed to get my grandmother to give me the piano that had been in her house for over forty years.

This piano was a wooden-framed (decent pianos are iron framed) upright which had been hand-painted white before decades of cigarette smoke had turned it a pale yellow.

Many of the keys didn't work and the ones that did were very out of tune and were impossible to fix.

On top of that we had to fit the piano into the tiny terrace house that I shared with my parents and three siblings.

I decided that I would start by teaching myself 'The Entertainer' by Scott Joplin.

If you haven't heard it, this is a quite complicated piece of 'ragtime' music from the early 1900s.

It took me about a year to learn the piece, which wasn't helped by the fact that my piano sounded terrible, by which time I dreamt that one day I would own a lovely (and in tune) piano.

Fast forward 25 years.

A big lorry pulled up outside my house and four men struggled to move an enormous wooden crate into my house.

An hour later I was sitting at the keyboard of my brand new Yamaha baby grand piano.

I played The Entertainer all the way through and realised that my dream had finally come true.

Both my daughters now play the piano because they have grown up hearing me play.

We've had many great singalongs and family get-togethers around the piano over the years.

While buying most material possessions doesn't usually deliver lasting happiness, buying a **dream** item, from which you will get very long-term use, can deliver a high level of sustained fulfilment.

It took me many years to be able to afford my dream piano, but it was well worth the wait and it continues to make me and my family very happy.

All other things being equal, working towards buying *your* dream item could do wonders for your personal motivation and long-term happiness and life satisfaction.

25

TIME GOES BY

WHY DELEGATION CAN BE A SMART IDEA

'It frees you from doing things you dislike. Since I dislike doing nearly everything, money is handy.'

Groucho Marx, American writer, comedian, stage, film and television star

A few years ago my garage roof was seriously in need of re-felting to stop rain penetrating.

I decided that this was a job that I should try to do myself rather than hire a professional roofer.

I bought a few rolls of what I thought was the correct roof felt.

I clambered onto the roof and quickly removed all the ripped and decayed old felt.

It then took me a few hours to remove all the felt nails that were protruding.

I struggled up the ladder with the first roll of felt, which felt like a bag of cement.

As I got level with the roof I threw the roll onto the roof.

I then started to push the roll up the roof, while still standing on the ladder.

Despite the ladder standing on soft grass, the bottom of the ladder slid backwards, as the heavy roll refused to move up the roof.

My legs went through the ladder rung as the ladder fell to the ground and the rung landed on one of my shins as my entire body landed on the ladder.

Blood was pouring from my leg and the pain was unbearable.

The next day I rang a roofer.

He came and did the whole job in half a day, using much thicker, larger felt, which he heated up with a gas burner.

The job cost me £350.

I was lucky not to break my shin bone and it took two weeks before I could walk properly and a month before I was fully recovered and could go running and do weight training again.

In hindsight I should have just hired the roofer to do the job for me in the first place.

Apart from avoiding the injury, discomfort and disruption to my exercise routine (which contributes to my happiness), I would have freed up the time to do things that I enjoy and which leverage my skills and experience.

There are many things that we can all do for ourselves, but a recent study suggests increased financial well-being from outsourcing things we don't like doing.

'People who hire a housecleaner or pay the kid next door to mow the lawn might feel like they're being lazy,' said study lead author Dr Ashley Whillans, assistant professor at Harvard Business School who carried out the research. 'But our results suggest that buying time has similar benefits for happiness as having more money.'

The researchers surveyed more than 6,000 adults in the United States, Denmark, Canada and the Netherlands.

'Money can in fact buy time. And it buys time pretty effectively,' said Professor Elizabeth Dunn, a psychology professor at the University of British Columbia, Canada, who worked on the study.

'In a series of surveys we find that people who spend money to buy themselves more free time ... have higher life satisfaction.

'Lots of research has shown that people benefit from buying their way into pleasant experiences, but our research suggests people should also consider buying their way out of unpleasant experiences.'

Professor Dunn also pointed out that the benefits of that extra time 'aren't just for wealthy people'.

'We thought the effects might only hold up for people with quite a bit of disposable income, but to our surprise, we found the same effects across the income spectrum.

'And so my take home message is, "think about it; is there something you hate doing, that fills you with dread? Could you pay somebody else to do that for you?" If so, then science says that's a pretty good use of money.' [36]

I'm pleased to say I made a full recovery from my roofing folly, but I've learned my lesson – pay others to do jobs you hate or are no good at!

26

IT'S A KIND OF MAGIC

HOW SPENDING MONEY ON EXPERIENCES INCREASES LIFE SATISFACTION AND HAPPINESS

'I spent a lot of money on booze, birds and fast cars. The rest I just squandered.'

George Best, Footballer

In 1986 I was seventeen.

I socialised with a small group of schoolfriends.

One of our group, Andy, announced that he was going to arrange buying tickets for a concert to be held that summer by the rock band Queen.

While I was aware of Queen's music and thought it was OK I wasn't what would be described as a fan.

'How much is this ticket going to cost?' I asked Andy.

'It's only £15,' he replied.

'I'm not sure I can afford that to go and see a band I'm really not that bothered about.'

'INXS and Status Quo are the warm-up acts and Queen are brilliant live,' Andy countered.

'You'll always be able to earn another £15 in the future but you might never get a chance to attend a Queen concert,' he added.

My other friends all agreed with Andy that not going would be a very bad move on my part.

I reluctantly agreed to pay for a ticket for me and my girlfriend at the time.

A few months later it was the day of the concert.

We travelled up to London's Wembley stadium on a lovely warm sunny Saturday.

The concert started at 4pm with INXS's lead singer Michael Hutchence belting out their song 'Same Direction'.

After INXS came Status Quo, playing a succession of their well known hits.

Then the stage went dark. Dry ice started to bellow across and the introduction for Queen's song 'One Vision' started to build.

Then the band exploded and Queen's lead singer, Freddie Mercury started to sing 'One man, one goal...'

The performance the band gave for the next two hours was nothing short of amazing.

The songs were brilliant, the musicianship was superb, the stage (and video screen) was enormous, the sound system (one of the loudest in history) was incredible.

I left that concert feeling that I had witnessed music history and from that moment onwards I became a big Queen fan.

But that tour was to be the original band's last as sadly, five years later, Freddie Mercury died of an Aids-related illness.

I have a DVD of that concert from 12th July 1986 and every few years I watch it and relive that amazing night.

The last time I watched it was with my two daughters on holiday, when I bored them senseless with my reminiscing of that day.

But the key point I made was that I am incredibly grateful that I had the chance to experience Queen live, in their heyday, and that using money to buy amazing life experiences like that have made me much happier than buying possessions or other 'stuff' ever could.

Research into happiness supports the idea that spending money on experiences generates more lasting joy than buying material things, because the emotional connection with the experience can be recounted for many years.[37]

So if you want to maximise your happiness you need to spend less on things and more on experiences.

Do this and you'll be able to say about your life: 'It's a kind of magic'*.

---

* 'A kind of magic' is a Queen song from their 1986 album of the same which they played during their 1986 'The Magic Tour' concerts.

27
WHO ARE YOU?

WHY YOU NEED TO MATCH SPENDING TO YOUR PERSONALITY

'All I ask is the chance to prove that money can't make me happy.'

Spike Milligan, British-Irish comedian, writer, musician, poet, playwright and actor

When I ran my financial services business I visited the firm's office in Central London a few days each week.

Because I live in rural Suffolk my travel involved a short drive to the station and then an hour on the train.

The frequency of my trips made it more cost-effective to pay for the car parking at the station on the day of my travel rather than buying an annual season ticket.

Several years ago the parking company introduced a smartphone app to pay for parking as an alternative to hanging about at the ticket machine to pay by change or card.

I would therefore park my car, board the train and then pay for my parking via the app. So far so good.

But every now and then I would have a problem. Sometimes I couldn't get a signal or the app froze.

And sometimes I got chatting to someone I knew and completely forgot to pay for the parking.

When I returned to my car that evening, there it was, slapped across the driver's side of the windscreen – a ticket.

The ticket was stuck on with industrial strength glue that made it almost impossible to remove.

Invariably I would spend 10 minutes trying to clear the gunge from the windscreen.

Whatever type of day I had had, seeing that I had been given a ticket, and the associated financial fine, made me very, very annoyed and deeply unhappy.

Apart from the financial implications, which I viewed as a terrible waste of hard-earned money, it was the negative feelings these occasional parking tickets evoked in me which were so painful.

And it seems that the reason for this extreme reaction is down to my personality.

Research from Cambridge University shows a link between different types of spending and personality types.[38]

The study, which was conducted in conjunction with a major UK bank, was based on the spending habits of 625 bank customers.

Each participant was asked to complete a standard personality and happiness questionnaire, and to consent to their responses being matched anonymously for research purposes with their bank transaction data.

A total of 76,863 spending transactions were then grouped by the bank into 59 categories that had at least 500 transactions over a six-month period.

The researchers matched spending categories on the "Big Five" personality traits – openness to experience (artistic versus traditional), conscientiousness (self-controlled vs easy-going), extraversion (outgoing vs reserved), agreeableness (compassionate vs competitive), and neuroticism (prone to stress vs stable).

CATEGORIES WITH THE LOWEST AND HIGHEST SCORES ON EACH OF THE BIG FIVE PERSONALITY TRAITS

THE BIG FIVE	LOW	HIGH
Openness to experience	Traffic fines, residential mortgages	Entertainment, hair and beauty
Conscientiousness	Gambling, toys and hobbies	Home insurance, health and fitness
Extraversion	Home insurance, accountant fees	Entertainment, travel
Agreeableness	Traffic fines, gambling	Charities, pets
Neuroticism	Stationery, hotels	Traffic fines, gambling

Source: Cambridge University

To identify which of the 'big five' personality types you are you can take a free online test – https://www.truity.com/test/big-five-personality-test – which takes only five minutes and there is no need to register or complete the political questions.

'Historically, studies had found a weak relationship between money and overall well-being,' says Joe Gladstone, one of the report's authors.

'Our study breaks new ground by mining actual bank-transaction data and demonstrating that spending can increase our happiness when it is spent on goods and services that fit our personalities and so meet our psychological needs.'

The researchers also backed up their findings by running a second experiment, where they gave people a voucher to spend in either a bookshop or at a bar.

Extroverts who were forced to spend at a bar were happier than introverts forced to spend at a bar, while introverts forced to spend at a bookshop were happier than extroverts forced to spend at a bookshop.

This follow-up experiment overcomes the limitations of correlational data by demonstrating that spending money on things that match a person's personality can cause an increase in happiness.

'Our findings suggest that spending money on products that help us express who we are as individuals could turn out to be as important to our well-being as finding the right job, the right neighbourhood or even the right friends and partners,' said Sandra Matz, another of the report's authors.

'By developing a more nuanced understanding of the links between spending and happiness, we hope to be able to provide more personalised advice on how to find happiness through the little consumption choices we make every day.'

So it seems that the more you align what you buy with what suits your personality, the more happiness you'll get for your money.

Buying the most comprehensive private health insurance might seem boring to an 'extraversion', however, if you're a 'conscientiousness' that might give you an equivalent level of happiness to their weekend in New York.

There must be something to this research because I haven't had a parking ticket for years now – the pain of a ticket is too great!

28

SWEET CHARITY

WHY SUPPORTING GOOD CAUSES IS GOOD FOR YOU

'No-one would remember the Good Samaritan if he'd only had good intentions; he had money as well.'

Margaret Thatcher, Former British Prime Minister

In the same year that I started my financial services business, two other big events happened to my wife and I.

We bought our family home – an old cottage in the country which needed a lot of work – and our first child was born.

The next few years were quite tough financially and cash was tight.

While we didn't live extravagantly we did have to be careful with our money.

One day I received something in the post from a homeless charity, setting out the challenges and problems faced by some people who had nowhere to live.

After reading the leaflet I felt very grateful to live in our lovely home, even if it was a bit tatty and in need of repair.

I also realised that there is always someone who has it worse than me.

But I also didn't want to make a donation to the homeless charity to assuage my guilty feelings arising from the donation request I had just received.

Even though we didn't have a high income at the time, I decided to start making a regular monthly contribution to a charity account and treat it as just another expense that had to be paid.

I then resolved to collect any charitable donation requests that came in the post and put them aside in a pile.

A few times a year I reviewed the pile and made an objective assessment as to which charities I would send a donation.

My simple decision formula for choosing which charities to donate to was to take 70% of the charity account and send an equal donation to one small, one big, one domestic and one international charity.

The remaining 30% left in the account was retained to enable us to make one-off donations to sponsor friends and relatives who were fundraising and also to emergency appeals.

Within a year of becoming more organised, systematic and intentional about charitable giving something amazing happened.

My business started to really take off, my income rose and I felt happier and had an even stronger sense of purpose and motivation.

Research suggests that planned charitable giving – known as pro-social giving – increases our overall happiness and well-being, particularly if it is to causes with which we have a personal connection.[39]

If you really can't afford to donate money then giving your time through volunteering can be just as good for your own well-being.

I'll never know whether those early regular charitable donations really did influence my own good fortune or if I would have been successful anyway.

What I do know is that they did and continue to contribute to my own sense of well-being and in that sense they were worth every penny.

BEING ON TRACK TO MEET YOUR FINANCIAL GOALS

CREATING AND UPDATING A FINANCIAL PLAN

29
CHARTING YOUR COURSE

MAKING DAILY DECISIONS IN THE CONTEXT OF LONG-TERM GOALS

*'If you don't know where you're going,
you'll end up someplace else.'*

Yogi Berra, American professional baseball catcher,
manager and coach

At 8am on 28th November 1979 Air New Zealand Flight 901 took off from Auckland International Airport with 257 people on board, destined for a sightseeing day trip to Antarctica.

However, the pilots were unaware that someone at Air New Zealand's flight control had changed the flight coordinates by two degrees.

This small change would take the plane 27 miles east of where the pilots thought they would be.

Unfortunately, the pilots did not have the right navigation charts on board to enable them to cross-check either the co-ordinates or their actual position at various waypoints during the flight.

After four hours, the plane approached Antarctica and the pilots descended to give the passengers a better view of the stunning landscapes.

Tragically, the incorrect co-ordinates had placed the plane in the path of active volcano Mount Erebus.

The snow on the volcano blended with the clouds above, making the pilots think that they were flying above flat ground.

By the time the instruments sounded the alarm it was too late and the plane crashed into the side of the volcano, killing all 257 people on board.

Setting the wrong flight coordinates by a small amount, failing to regularly cross-check the progress of the flight, combined with lack of visibility all led to a terrible catastrophe.

Planning your lifetime wealth is a bit like planning a long-distance plane journey.

You need to have an idea of where you are heading in terms of life expectancy, cash inflows and outflows, key life events and when you want to have achieved financial independence (that stage when paid work is optional – you work because you want to, not because you have to).

Along the way you'll need to make course corrections in the light of actual spending, income, taxes, inflation, and investment returns.

A recent study found that people who had a long-term financial plan experienced greater financial well-being. Thinking about their life over many years, rather than just the here and now gave them context for financial decisions and made them feel more in control of day-to-day spending, resulting in lower debt and higher savings.

'...we found that a person's perspective on time was far more influential than income, age, education, or gender when it came to personal finances. Our results showed that people who think further into the future tend to save more frequently and build larger savings balances in retirement and non-retirement accounts.

'Compared with those with time horizons of less than a year, people with full financial life plans had, on average, 20 times more money saved. Even looking ahead by just a few years increased savings fourfold.

'Our analyses showed time horizon had a significantly greater impact on economic behaviours than income. Yes, a person must have income that is adequate to their needs if they are going to be able to save. Our study suggests, however, that, regardless of paycheck size, having a future-oriented mindset can make the difference between allowing expenses to crowd out one's income or finding ways to save money.

'The lesson here is fascinating: A sense of personal power – not money itself – may be the key to emotional well-being in our financial lives.' [40]

As you progress along your plan you might decide that you need to save more, take more investment risks with your capital, work longer or release capital from your home by downsizing.

You might even decide to change course completely and head for a different destination as explained in chapter 31.

The key point is you make day-to-day decisions about spending and working in the context of the impact this is likely to have on your long-term financial position.

As I explain in chapter 30 your long-term future seems abstract and distant compared to the here-and-now but you can't ignore it.

Lots of daily spending, saving and investing decisions quickly add up to have a big impact on your long-term financial security.

Plotting your financial course, in the form of a basic lifetime financial forecast of cashflow and liquid wealth, will help you to make better financial decisions with which you can live.

30

MY GENERATION

WHY YOU NEED TO GET TO KNOW THE OLDER YOU

'It's difficult to make forecasts, especially about the future.'

Samuel Goldwyn, Polish-American film producer

David was my best friend at infant and junior schools.

We did start at the same secondary school, but David's parents removed him after the first year as they realised how bad it was and wanted a better education for him.

David became a pupil at a prestigious (and expensive) independent school and we gradually drifted apart.

Over twenty years later I was reading a financial services newspaper and saw comments attributed to someone who had the same name as my old school friend.

David has a very unusual surname and I had never seen anyone else with that name.

I wondered whether the David mentioned in the article could be my old chum.

I rang the company that David represented and left my name and number and asked him to return my call.

A few days later I received a call and sure enough he was my old schoolfriend. We agreed to meet up a few weeks later.

The last time I had seen David was when he was twelve, with a mop of jet black hair and a cheeky smile.

I was quite shocked to meet a man in his mid-thirties with grey-flecked hair and lines around his eyes.

David looked fit and healthy but I was taken aback to see him as a man.

All those years ago, when we had last seen each other, I could never have envisaged how he would look nearly 25 years later.

This inability to envisage ourselves in the long-term future can have serious implications for our financial well-being.

To support yourself when you can't or don't want to work in old age you need to save diligently and regularly now. You need to resist the impulse to spend all of your income as you earn it.

But we are naturally programmed to discount the future.

Retirement, being a rather abstract and vague issue, *feels* so far away and there are so many things you could enjoy right now which are more tangible and vivid!

Psychologists call this situation *psychological distance*.

This can make it very hard to forgo spending on things that give immediate reward in order to save for your retirement or other long-term goals.

One way to reduce impulsive spending and make your future feel more real and important is to have a clear picture of your future self.

Research by Dr. Hal Hershfield shows that people who interacted with a detailed avatar of their future self made more patient financial decisions.

'Specifically, when the future self shares similarities with the present self, when it is viewed in vivid and realistic terms, and when it is seen in a positive light, people are more willing to make choices today that may benefit them at some point in the years to come.'[41]

One way to reduce the *psychological distance* between your present and future self is to use one of the many age-progression applications to create a vivid picture of how you might look in 20 or 30 years' time.

My personal favourite age progression app is AgingBooth as it's free, easy to use and available on Android and Apple systems, but there are many others that you can use.

Although looking at your future self is a bit weird initially, it does make the long-term seem much less far away and easier to comprehend.

The chances are you will live a very long life.

Regularly looking at a picture of the future you might help you make the right saving choices so you can afford to enjoy all of it.

31

AS CLEAR AS MUD

WHY YOU DON'T NEED TO GET HUNG UP ON HAVING CLEAR FINANCIAL GOALS

'I have enough money to last me the rest of my life, provided I die tomorrow.'

Johnny Bush, singer, songwriter and drummer

A few months after my wife and I first met we decided that we wanted to go on a foreign holiday together.

We both liked France but we couldn't decide exactly where to go, or what type of accommodation to stay at.

We therefore decided to buy a ferry ticket for our car, a map of France, and a copy of The Good Hotel Guide.

Then we headed off to Dover for the crossing to France to see where that took us.

When we got to France we looked at the map and agreed that we wanted to head south, but we were prepared to be flexible and take an indirect route through the country.

For our first stop we found a small town about fifteen minutes' drive from the motorway and located in our guide book a farm which had small apartments.

Luckily they had a room which was free that night so we set off.

On the way we stopped for a pleasant lunch and a walk around a small village.

We got to the farm about 4pm and were welcomed by the farmer and his family.

The apartment was lovely and nearby was a private open-air swimming pool which we were invited to use to cool off given it was a very warm, sunny day.

The next day we left and made our way to Paris and found a lovely little hotel on the outskirts and spent a few days exploring the city.

Then we moved on to the south-east and found a hotel in a pretty village.

The hotel itself was very gothic and unusual and the female couple who ran it were eccentric and extremely funny.

Each day we looked at the map and rang around until we found available accommodation and then set off.

There was only one day when we couldn't find any accommodation, which meant we had to sleep in our car, but it wasn't too bad.

That holiday we didn't have a clear plan of where we wanted to go. Our goal was just to spend two weeks together in France, be flexible and have lots of different experiences.

We still remember that holiday and how much we enjoyed it, which was far more than many holidays where we had a clear plan and destination.

For many people 'Goals' is a loaded word.

Most of us don't really know what we want to do in the future.

For some the long-term means five years; for others it means 50 years.

No-one wants to think about getting older, but why not think about being younger for longer?

People don't have financial goals: they have life goals which may have a financial implication.

The key is to work out what 'good' looks like – where you think you might want to be in five, ten, twenty and 30 years' time.

In my experience few people have concrete life goals, they have what financial adviser and author Carl Richards calls 'guesses'.

'Don't get overwhelmed thinking about the future – relax and just make some guesses.

'We're more interested in the process of guessing and trying to be less wrong,' says Carl.

'You might think: I want to go this way, now I want to go this way, and what about this way?'

A person born in the developed world today has a 50% chance of living to 105 and this age has been increasing steady at the rate of two years every decade.[42]

Increasing longevity means you need to be adaptable, flexible and invest in both intangible assets (health, well-being, skills, education, relationships) and tangible financial assets (savings, investments and property).

Financial planning is a process, not a one-time event or static written document and it is the thinking behind the process that is important, particularly in the context of a very long life.

Or, as Carl Richards says, 'The financial plan is dead, long live financial planning!'[43]

32

RETREAT FROM SOCIETY

WHY YOU MIGHT NOT WANT TO RETIRE

"I'm not chasing youthfulness. I'm chasing health. People have been brainwashed to think that after you're 65, you're finished. But retirement is a financial disaster and a health catastrophe."

Charles Eugster, indoor 200m and outdoor 400m sprint world record holder for men over 95

Reg Buttress started work at thirteen as a coal miner's assistant in South Wales in 1937.

When the local mine closed Reg moved to Birmingham to work in various factories until they were bombed in the Second World War.

Reg then moved back to South Wales where he got a job as a fireman on a steam train.

Some years later Reg progressed to driving trains, which he did until he was made redundant in 1964 when his depot closed.

Reg then re-invented himself as a machinist for industrial chemicals group ICI, where he trained others until he was made redundant in 1979 aged 56,

Despite being unemployed for two years, Reg eventually got a job as a checkout operator at J Sainsbury's, the supermarket chain.

In 1988, when he reached age 65, Reg retired from Sainsbury's but after just six weeks he felt bored and asked for his old job back.

When asked why he wasn't retired Reg said: 'You've got to stay active to stay alive. I love my job and want to keep doing it for as long as I can."

Despite the death of his wife in 2011, Reg finally found love again when he met Ruth in 2014.

Reg stayed at Sainsbury's for a total of 29 years after his first 'retirement' until his 'final' retirement at age 95 in autumn 2017, which was seven years later than his son Michael's retirement in 2010.

Reg clearly found a lot of purpose in his work, and he obviously did it for so long because he enjoyed it, not because he needed the money.

Maintaining purpose in life has been shown to be a significant factor in overall well-being and longevity, and for many people work gives them that purpose.

A study of people in their sixties in the US, UK and Europe found a strong link between early retirement and a reduction in mental capability (known as cognitive decline).[44]

Another study of US adults concluded that there may be a link between early retirement and early death and, conversely, that retiring later might lead to a longer life.[45]

The United Nations estimates that globally, the number of those aged 60 or over will more than double by 2050 and more than triple by the end of this century.[46]

In their groundbreaking book – The 100 Year-Life – London Business School professors Lynda Gratton and Andrew Scott point out that '...if you are now twenty you have a 50 per cent chance of living to more than 100; if you are 40 you have an evens chance of reaching 95; if you are 60, then a 50 per cent chance of making 90 or more.'[47]

Against the backdrop of people living much longer, Gratton and Scott argue that the traditional "three-stage life" concept of education followed by work and then retirement will be unfeasible and financially unviable for many people.

If living to 100 becomes the norm then one consequence is that we will have to work longer to accumulate sufficient financial resources and also to reduce and defer the time at which we need to draw on those assets.

Gratton and Scott also content that we will need to constantly retrain and reinvent ourselves to stay ahead of technology and the demand for changing skill-sets in order to remain a productive member of the workforce.

So while working for longer, but perhaps less intensely and with more than one career, looks like being necessary for our financial well-being, it can also be good for our mental health.

33

PENNIES FROM HEAVEN

WHY FREE MONEY IS A NO-BRAINER

*'Son, if you really want something in this life,
you have to work for it. Now quiet! They're about
to announce the lottery numbers.'*

Homer Simpson

Over the years I have, from time to time, given pro bono guidance to people who wouldn't otherwise be able to afford my fees.

Some years ago a middle-aged lady came to see me for help in working out whether she should accept her employer's redundancy offer.

The lump sum on offer was certainly large and the lady was tempted to accept the offer and retire.

I reviewed a summary of the lady's assets, liabilities and expenditure.

'Where is your pension statement?' I asked her.

The lady passed over some papers.

'No, this is your State pension forecast, what I want to see is your company pension benefit statement.'.

'Well I'm not in the company pension scheme because I opted out when I first joined as I didn't think I could afford the contribution,' the lady answered.

'How long have you worked there?' I asked.

The lady thought for a moment and then answered 'About twenty years, I think.'

'So you've not been accruing pension benefits for the past twenty years?' I asked incredulously.

'Yes,' she said sheepishly.

'But surely you could have afforded to have joined since then?'

'Well…yes but I just never got round to completing the paperwork.'

The lady's employer's pension scheme was extremely generous and in return for her paying 6% of her salary she would have built up a pension entitlement of about a third of her salary, had she joined it all those years ago.

The actual cost of that pension benefit was a lot more than the 6% contribution the lady would have had to pay – in fact it was in the region of 30% of her salary.

The upshot was that her State pension entitlement and income from the lump sum wouldn't be enough to enable her to retire, or at least not to support her desired lifestyle.

'Either you don't take redundancy and instead immediately join your company pension scheme and pay as much in as you can, or you do take the redundancy money and invest it and hope to be able to get a new job and pension scheme on similar terms,' I told her.

The lady ended up being made compulsorily redundant a few months later anyway and she struggled to find a new job that paid anything like she was used to earning. She had to make some big changes to her lifestyle.

Most developed countries now have rules that mean employers have to automatically enrol their staff in a suitable pension scheme and make a certain level of contribution in return for employees also making a modest contribution.

This is effectively free money because if you don't join the pension scheme the employer won't pay you their contribution as extra salary.

Say you contributed £160 and your employer added £100 – that would be an effective immediate return of over 62%!

If you have 'bad' debt that needs repaying first then it might make sense to deal with that before making personal contributions to a pension, but otherwise getting the employer's matching contributions will be hugely beneficial.

Getting that 'free' money regularly over a long period of time, together with investment returns (which is explained in chapter 35), will enable you to build a meaningful pot of money with which you can fund your lifestyle when you can't or no longer wish to work for money.

34

A SURE BET

WHY MORTGAGE REPAYMENTS CAN BE A GREAT INVESTMENT

'A bank is a place that will lend you money if you can prove that you don't need it.'

Bob Hope, Actor and entertainer

I bought my first home in late 1989.

I paid £62,000 for it and borrowed £58,000 (i.e. a mortgage), which is equivalent in today's money to about £153,000 and £143,000 respectively at the time of writing (August 2017).

By the time I moved in to the property mortgage interest rates had started to rise and the UK economy started moving into a dramatic slowdown.

By early 1991 the value of my home had fallen to about £55,000 and interest rates were at an all-time high.

My mortgage was a repayment type, meaning that as long as I paid the monthly payment the loan would be repaid after 25 years.

With a repayment mortgage most of the monthly payment represents interest on the loan and only a tiny amount is a repayment of the amount borrowed.

This means that it takes many years for the outstanding loan balance to start falling by a meaningful amount.

I decided that it made a lot of sense to start overpaying my monthly mortgage payments, which I started doing at the rate of £500 per month.

It was my choice to do this. I wasn't obligated to continue as the term of the mortgage hadn't been changed (a shorter repayment period would have caused the repayments to increase).

The main benefit of overpaying each month was that I reduced the outstanding mortgage at a much quicker rate than would have otherwise been the case, thereby reducing the chance of owing more than the property was worth when I came to sell it.

The second benefit was that I was effectively obtaining a risk free, tax free return on my money of about 16% per annum. This was because mortgage rates at the time were about 12% and I was a 25% taxpayer.

Had I instead saved the mortgage overpayments in a deposit account it would need to pay gross interest of 16% so that after deduction of 25% income tax I would end up with a 12% return.

I eventually sold my apartment in 1994 for £44,000, which was a loss of £18,000.

Thankfully my overpayments had reduced the mortgage balance to about £42,000 by then, allowing me to move on.

Global interest rates are currently at an all-time low, which has pushed up property values and caused lots of people to take on very high levels of debt, including mortgages.

Mortgage debt is currently cheap and property values are high by historical standards – but it may not stay that way.

History tells us that booms turn to busts and bubbles eventually burst, leaving a wave of wealth-destruction in their wake.

Assuming you've got no 'bad debt' (see chapter five), you have an adequate cash emergency fund (see chapter 16), and you are receiving the maximum employer contributions to any workplace pension scheme (see chapter 33) overpaying your mortgage makes a lot of sense.

The fact that mortgage costs are low just means that overpayments will reduce the loan outstanding even quicker, thereby building more equity in your home.

A lower loan-to-property value might also enable you to qualify for a cheaper mortgage, thereby enabling you to reduce your loan balance even quicker.

When the cost of debt is low it is tempting to spend more of your income on living today, rather than repaying your mortgage as quickly as possible.

When the cost of debt rises then so do your monthly repayments, so if you pay more than you contractually need to now, you'll reduce the impact when rates do go up.

Clearing your mortgage quickly isn't something other people can see, in the same way as nice clothes, smart cars, or other 'things', but it can certainly make you feel more secure and that will increase your sense of financial well-being.

35

ASTRONOMY NOT ASTROLOGY

HOW TO CAPTURE YOUR FAIR SHARE OF INVESTMENT RETURNS

'Don't look for the needle in the haystack.
Just buy the haystack!'

John "Jack" C. Bogle, American investor,
business magnate and philanthropist

Some years ago Gloria asked me for some advice on her financial situation.

Gloria had been widowed 25 years earlier when she was 45, when her husband Greg died while on active service in the UK army.

In addition to a widow's pension Gloria was given a £250,000 lump sum.

Gloria's main objective was generating a sensible income from her capital so she could continue to live comfortably.

On the advice of a stockbroker who had been introduced by her solicitor, Gloria agreed to invest her capital into a portfolio of gilts (lending money to the government for a fixed rate of interest).

The gilt portfolio initially provided an initial income of £20,000 per annum and Gloria was very happy.

By the time Gloria consulted me she was concerned that her income had been falling over the years and was now £15,000 per annum a reduction magnified by the impact of inflation.

The capital value of the portfolio had remained static at about £250,000 as gilts matured and were reinvested.

I estimated that, had Gloria invested in a portfolio of 70% shares and 30% bonds at outset and had the income arising distributed to her each year, her annual income would have grown steadily and be about £60,000 per annum now and the portfolio value would have grown in value to about £1 million.

I explained to Gloria that, as she was in good health, she could probably expect to live for 20 to 25 years and as such her current gilt portfolio would continue to deliver less and less income and the portfolio would remain static.

I explained that she needed to re-arrange her portfolio to have some exposure to equities and possibly index-linked gilts to help protect her income and capital against inflation.

The price Gloria had to pay for this was a drop in initial income from £15,000 to £8,000 per annum.

Gloria was not prepared to accept the short-term pain of a drop in income and she decided to leave her portfolio as it was.

Many people fail to allocate their long-term savings to any or sufficient growth-oriented investments in the mistaken belief that they can't stomach short-term fluctuations in value.

This means that the capital generates lower returns in the long run, meaning a lower standard of living, higher amounts of regular savings or working for longer.

There are three basic principles of investing that you need to understand.

PRINCIPLE 1: RISK AND REWARD ARE RELATED.

The three principal investment asset classes are cash (liquid savings), bonds (a part share of a fixed rate loan to a government or company) and equities (a part share of the profits of a business).

Cash has the lowest capital risk and thus the lowest long-term expected return.

Bonds have more risk attached but less so than equities and thus offer potentially higher long-term returns than cash, but lower potential long-term returns than equities.

Equities are the riskiest, but also offer the highest potential long-term returns.

Companies' cost of capital (in the form of cash distributions they have to pay out to attract investors) is your return as an investor, and over the long-term capitalism tends to reward shareholders well through dividends and increasing share prices.

Risk, in the form of uncertain outcomes and potential loss of capital, is the source of returns, with higher risk generally associated with higher expected returns.

Always remember that there are no low risk/high return investments.

PRINCIPLE 2: WITH INVESTMENTS YOU GET EVERYTHING YOU DON'T PAY FOR.

You can get access to a well-diversified global investment portfolio fund for a fee of 0.25% per annum of the amount you invest.

Many investment funds charge between three to ten times what the cheapest funds charge on the basis that they might be able to beat the overall stockmarket.

Costs are certain but returns aren't and it makes no sense to pay any more than you have to in order to gain access to the stockmarket.

Index funds basically deliver the returns of the overall stockmarket, but at much lower costs than funds managed by clever people who try to outperform the market.

Jack Bogle is the founder of Vanguard, which with around £3 trillion is the second-largest mutual fund manager in the world. This is what he has to say about investing:

'The index fund is a most unlikely hero for the typical investor. It is no more (nor less) than a broadly diversified portfolio, typically run at rock-bottom costs, without the putative benefit of a brilliant, resourceful, and highly skilled portfolio manager. The index fund simply buys and holds the securities in a particular index, in proportion to their weight in the index. The concept is simplicity writ large.'[48]

So there really is no need to pay high annual charges to have your money managed by a manager who makes decisions on what companies to buy, when and how much. An index or tracker fund approach should be your default.

PRINCIPLE 3: DON'T PUT ALL YOUR INVESTMENT EGGS IN ONE BASKET.

Unless you are starting your own business, diversifying across asset classes and investing in a variety of companies lowers risk without lowering potential returns.

It makes no sense to invest in individual companies or sectors of the stockmarket (like Korean technology or European companies) because the potential returns are not sufficient to outweigh the much higher risks.

Abraham Okusanya is a UK-based investment researcher who has created the concept of the **No-Brainer** portfolio.

The idea is that the starting point for the asset allocation of your portfolio should be based on how investors across the world allocate capital across different types of financial assets as shown in the pie chart below.[49]

GLOBAL MARKET PORTFOLIO

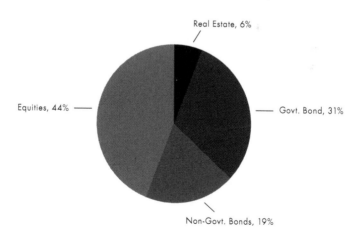

Doeswijk, Ronald Q. and Lam, Trevin and Swinkels, Laurens,
Historical Returns of the Market Portfolio (June 1 2017)

This equates to a portfolio with 50% invested in bonds and 50% in equities.

However, given that each investor has their own risk preference, they can increase or decrease the equity content within their portfolio.

So we end up with five no-brainer portfolios, depending on the risk the investor is prepared to take, as shown below.[50]

THE 'NO-BRAINER' PORTFOLIOS

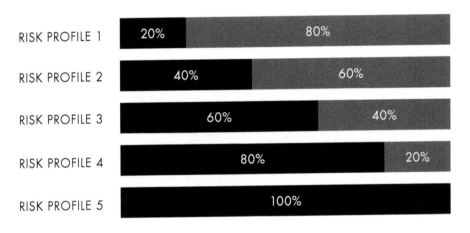

Fund groups like Vanguard with their Lifestrategy range, and Blackrock with their Consensus range, offer very low cost, globally diversified portfolios with a choice of risk and reward profiles, for an annual charge of around 0.25% per annum of the amount you invest.

So, in summary, get broad stockmarket exposure that meets your risk/reward profile, keep costs low (I personally use a multi-index portfolio fund) and take a very long-term view,

But I'll leave the last word to Warren Buffett, one of the most successful investors of all time and one of the richest people in the world.

'In investing, it is not necessary to do extraordinary things to get extraordinary results.'

36

BRICK BY BRICK

ONE WAY TO PLUG YOUR RETIREMENT INCOME BLACK HOLE

*'He made his money the really old-fashioned way.
He inherited it.'*

A. J. Carothers, American playwright and television writer

In 2008 Jessica Bruno and her husband Tony were looking for a new home but couldn't find anything that suited.

As a temporary measure they and their son Tony junior moved in with Jessica's parents at their home in Sutton, a small town in Massachusetts.

Jessica grew up in this home and she has fond memories of a happy childhood which included her parents having an open house for any of Jessica's and her brother's friends who had issues at home.

Several months after Jessica and her family moved in, her grandparents (her father's parents) also moved in.

All four generations have lived under the same roof ever since.[51]

And if that wasn't enough, Jessica, her father and grandfather all work together refurbishing other people's homes!

'At the end of the day, all you really have is family,' Tony Bruno told ABC News. 'When we're all here together, it's what's important. I am pretty grateful I have this.'

Having four generations of a family in one home might not be right for everyone. As well as being able to get along you also need a big enough house.

Even if you don't want to share your home with other family generations, you might still want enough room for them to come and stay regularly.

You might also value the opportunity to have regular family gatherings.

You may also have strong emotional attachment to your home and like the areas in which you live, with friends and relatives nearby.

The reality for many older people, however, is that they often need to sell their family home and move into something smaller to release some of the equity to help fund their later life.

As well as losing valuable space for family visits, selling can present a whole series of other problems:

- The costs and associated taxes of buying and selling.
- Finding a suitable property in the same area.
- Funding refurbishment and repair of the new property.
- The upheaval and hassle of moving.

It is for these types of scenarios that lifetime mortgages are designed, for those aged 55 and over.

You borrow a proportion of the property's value, typically below 50%.

The interest on the loan is fixed and rolls up until you or your executors sell the property and repay the outstanding amount.

This means that the loan amount will increase over time, although the lender guarantees you will never owe more than the property's value.

This means that the potential legacy to your heirs is likely to be much less, assuming that you spend the equity released from the original loan.

For example a £65,000 loan with rolled up annual interest of 6.4% per annum would grow to £137,000 after twelve years[*]

If you need more cash to plug a shortfall in your retirement resources, but don't want to move home, a lifetime mortgage might be right for you.

Just make sure that you don't make your home too inviting and comfortable or you might end up with family guests who never leave!

---

[*] Consumer organisation Which? has a great short video which explains the pros and cons of equity release which you can view at http://www.which.co.uk/money/pensions-and-retirement/youre-retired-working-on-benefits-equity-release/guides/equity-release/what-is-equity-release

37

A PLACE FOR EVERYTHING

KNOWING WHAT YOU HAVE AND WHERE IT IS

'My mother says I didn't open my eyes for eight days after I was born, but when I did, the first thing I saw was an engagement ring. I was hooked.'

Elizabeth Taylor, British actress

Arthur was a Second World War veteran who went on to become involved in a range of business activities for the rest of his life.

He died aged 87, surviving his wife by 15 years.

Arthur's daughter and son, Sarah and Gerald, had the task of dealing with Arthur's financial affairs after his death.

After hours of searching they found his will.

They also found piles of papers – statements, letters and certificates – scattered around his large rambling house.

After the best part of a week Sarah and Gerald had uncovered hundreds of documents relating to what they thought Arthur owned and slowly started to create a list.

This list included 22 savings accounts, 34 listed shares, 46 investment funds, seven life insurance policies, twelve National Savings & Investments' holdings, details of three other properties and a piece of land.

Then Sarah and Gerald had to write to all the various organisations to advise them of Arthur's death.

A few weeks later, during a conversation with Arthur's brother, Sarah and Gerald learnt that Arthur also owned a minority shareholding in a successful small business.

After investigation it transpired that the business was paying Arthur an annual dividend of £30,000.

The company's other shareholders agreed to buy Arthur's shares for £400,000!

All in all it took about a year for Sarah and Gerald to untangle Arthur's financial affairs and they were still finding assets months after compiling their first asset inventory.

When a person dies someone has to deal with their financial affairs. This means identifying what the deceased person owned and owed.[*]

But, as Arthur's story illustrates, this is sometimes easier said than done.

In the UK there is a free service to help track down 'lost' accounts and savings – http://www.mylostaccount.org.uk/ – but it is time-consuming and not always successful.

It also doesn't help track down investments, land or buildings that the person owned.

---

[*] Consumer organisation Which? Has a useful explanation of what to do when someone dies on their website. https://www.moneyadviceservice.org.uk/en/categories/when-someone-dies

Financial data firm Experian provides an Unclaimed Assets Register https://www.uar.co.uk/ to help track down lost assets but again this is time-consuming and not foolproof.

That's why it's essential to maintain an up-to-date list of your assets and liabilities, together with contact details and, where appropriate, account numbers.

As well as physical and financial assets, your asset inventory should also include details of your digital assets, including social media accounts.

Take time to update your asset inventory each year as part of your personal financial checkup.

Passing away need not mean passing on a mess to your nearest and dearest, but passing on the benefit of your hard work in the form of a nice tidy list.

38

WILL POWER

HOW TO POTENTIALLY LIVE EIGHT YEARS LONGER

*'I made my money the old-fashioned way.
I was very nice to a wealthy relative right before he died'*

Malcolm Forbes, American entrepreneur

Elderly Lisbon resident Helena was surprised one day when she was contacted by a Portuguese law firm who advised her that she was one of the beneficiaries of Luis Carlos, a recently deceased Portuguese aristocrat.

Helena was surprised because she had never heard of Luis Carlos.

Luis Carlos de Noronha Cabral de Camara was the illegitimate son of a wealthy Portuguese aristocrat.

When he died aged 42 as a childless bachelor, his estate comprised a twelve-bedroom apartment in Lisbon, another property in the country, a car and about €25,000 cash.

Many years before his death Luis had made a will in which he had named 70 people as equal beneficiaries of his estate.

But the strange thing was that Luis had chosen his beneficiaries at random from the Lisbon telephone directory.

Given the number of surviving beneficiaries, each one only ended up receiving several thousand Euros, but as an unexpected windfall it was still a pleasant surprise.

It seems that Luis was motivated to leave his estate to random strangers because there were no charities that he felt were worthy of his money and, in the absence of direct descendants, his wealth would otherwise have passed to the Portuguese state.

If you don't make a will your assets will be dealt with according to the rules of succession in the jurisdiction in which you live or, in some cases, where the asset is located.

Making a will enables you to say what you want to happen to your wealth and personal possessions after your death, including who gets what and how much.

In most countries making a will reduces the time it takes to deal with a deceased person's affairs. Sometimes having a will enables the estate to reduce or avoid paying estate taxes.

But it seems one of the best reasons for making a will is that it might help you push back the day of your last breath by quite a few years.

In the UK the average age at death of people without a will is about 78.

The average age at death for people with a will is about 82 – an extra four years.

The average age at death for people with a will which also includes a charitable request is 84 – an extra total of six year years over the no-will people!

Interestingly, the average will is made four years and one month prior to the individual's death.

So perhaps if you redo your will every four years you'll live forever!

39

RULES OF THE ROAD

LEGACIES THAT LAST

'Inherited wealth is a real handicap to happiness. It is as certain a death to ambition as cocaine is to morality.'

William K. Vanderbilt, grandson of Cornelius Vanderbilt

In 1810 Cornelius "Commodore" Vanderbilt, aged sixteen, used $100 borrowed from his mother to set up a passenger boat on Staten Island in New York.

By all accounts Cornelius was a hard-driving, rough character.

A Vanderbilt descendant described him as 'illiterate, bad-tempered and foul-mouthed, and inclined, when trapped into a social event, to spit streams of tobacco juice and fondle the maids.'

A more recent review of American history described him in kinder terms. 'While Vanderbilt could be a rascal, combative and cunning, he was much more a builder than a wrecker. ... being honourable, shrewd, and hard-working.

Cornelius expanded his business into the steamboat business and then built a railroad empire.

After marrying his cousin they went on to have 13 children.

A year after Cornelius's wife's died – when he was 75 – he married a cousin 43 years his junior.

When he died at age 82, Cornelius was worth $100 million dollars (over $150 billion in today's money) – more than was held in the U.S. Treasury at the time.

Cornelius left most of his fortune to his eldest son William as he felt he was the most capable of continuing business success.

William died only nine years later, by which time he had more than doubled his inheritance to $230 million (over $300 billion today).

The bulk of his wealth was left to his two sons, Cornelius and William.

Members of the Vanderbilt family went on to build a number of opulent houses and ended up dominating prime real estate in New York's Manhattan district.

They gave money away to high profile charities, held extravagant parties and raced yachts, sportscars, and horses.

Yet within less than 30 years of the death of the Commodore, no member of the Vanderbilt family was among the richest in the U.S., and just 48 years after his death, one of his grandchildren is thought to have died penniless.

The Vanderbilts held a family reunion at Vanderbilt University in 1973 attended by 120 family members. Not one of them was a millionaire.

In less than one generation the Vanderbilt family had spent the majority of their family wealth and it was virtually all gone within four generations.

Descendants have explained that the absence of any structure or organization in the way the family transferred wealth from one generation to the next was the main cause of the inability to preserve that wealth.[52]

Put simply the family members went from producers of great wealth to great consumers of it.

Research suggests that 90% of inherited wealth is depleted by the third generation.

A combination of property, pension and business wealth means that it isn't difficult to end up leaving several hundred thousand pounds, and increasingly people can expect to pass on several million pounds, dollars or Euros of wealth.

Most people who have accumulated significant wealth did so not by inheriting but through a mixture of hard work and rises in asset values over the past few decades.

One way to increase the chances of preserving family wealth, particularly where the amount is significant, and ensure that it is not a negative influence on the younger generation, is to develop and articulate a clear idea of the purpose of that wealth and to ensure that it is clearly understood.

Obviously, the main objective will be to provide the desired lifestyle for family members without that leading to extravagance or over-indulgence.

Financial capital is just one of the three elements of family wealth, with the other two being human capital (each family member's time, skills, experience, knowledge and labour) and intellectual capital (each family member's ability to develop wisdom and understanding).

Wealth-succession experts Roy Williams and Vic Preisser have created a ten-point wealth transition checklist to help families evaluate their wealth transition plan, and this is reproduced below.

WEALTH TRANSITION CHECKLIST[53]
(WRITTEN AS POSITIVE AFFIRMATIONS RATHER THAN AS QUESTIONS)

1.	Our family has a mission statement that spells out the overall purpose of our wealth.
2.	The entire family is involved in the most important decisions, such as defining a mission for our wealth.
3.	All family heirs have the option of participating in the management of the family's assets.
4.	Heirs understand their future roles, have "bought into" those roles, and look forward to performing those roles.
5.	Heirs have actually reviewed the family's estate plans and documents.
6.	Our current wills, trusts, and other documents make most asset-distributions based on heir readiness, not heir age.
7.	Our family mission includes creating incentives and opportunities for our heirs.
8.	Our younger children are encouraged to participate in our family's philanthropic grant-making decisions.
9.	Our family considers family unity to be just as important as financial strength.
10.	We communicate well throughout our family and regularly meet as a family to discuss issues and changes.

Whatever your net worth, developing effective communication, trust and understanding within your family will maximise the chance of any wealth you leave being a force for good for many generations to come.

WALKING THE TALK

TIME TO TAKE ACTION

40

FINANCIAL WELL-BEING CHEAT SHEET

MINDSET, BEHAVIOURS, HABITS AND ACTIONS

'The path to success is to take massive, determined actions.'

Tony Robbins, American author, entrepreneur, philanthropist and life coach.

To help you apply the concepts and ideas set out earlier, here is a simple list of habits and actions to help increase your overall financial wellbeing.

1. Regularly tell yourself 'I am good with money and I am master of my own destiny'. Remind yourself that there is an abundance of wealth, not scarcity, and you can and will build enough wealth to meet your needs. This simple mindset can help you to see opportunities rather than challenges, and solutions rather than problems.

2. Every time you are about to make a purchase ask yourself *'Do I really need this and will it make me happy, more secure and increase my financial freedom?'* Learning to say *'Yes'* less and *'No'* more to potential spending is the key to feeling in control and spending less.

3. Remember there is no such thing as a sale or 'must buy by' date. There are only sales promotions designed to manipulate you into buying today. Remind yourself that you will have to answer to your future self for the actions you take today.

4. Try to avoid using contactless card payments for daily small purchases. Instead take out a set amount of cash for the week and use that as it will make the spending more tangible and will reduce the potential to make impulse purchases. Learning to control lots of small spending actions on a daily basis will increase your overall financial wellbeing.

5. Ask yourself *'What need am I trying to meet'* with every proposed purchase and *'Can I meet this need without spending?'* This simple approach can help you reduce spending.

6. Understand where your money goes by downloading your bank transactions to a spreadsheet or creating a written budget from receipts and bank statements. Look for ways to reduce spending on phone/broadband/entertainment, energy, insurance and debt costs. Look for ways to stop spending on subscriptions, memberships, eating out and clothes.

7. Remember to pay yourself first, in the form of saving to your emergency fund, long term investing and debt reduction. *You* should be the first bill you pay.

8. Never compare your lifestyle, possessions or social status to others. There will always be someone who has more than you.

9. The best investment you can ever make is in yourself in terms of improved skills, knowledge, understanding, and communication skills. Increasing your annual income by £2,000 per annum is more effective than trying to save 30p on your daily coffee.

10. Never go shopping (physical or online) when you feel sad or depressed. You are more likely to spend more and buy things you don't need.

11. Always remember that income comes from your own resources – time, energy and skills – not your employer. If you lose your job you haven't lost your resources.

12. Avoid using overdrafts, credit cards, catalogue clubs, store cards or car loans to finance spending. These are **bad debts** that are very expensive and will hold you back from becoming financially secure.

13. Build an emergency fund of between 3 – 12 months' expenditure to enable you meet unexpected expenses.

14. As a general rule, do not opt out of your employer's pension scheme and make sure that you contribute as much as is necessary (and you can afford) to qualify for the maximum contribution from your employer. This is effectively **free** money.

15. On regular occasions declutter your home (and garage/shed) and sell, give away or recycle your unwanted possessions. This will help reduce your desire to spend and help you to feel more in control of your finances.

16. Create and regularly update a list of your physical, financial and digital assets so you know exactly what you have and, more importantly, your next of kin does too.

17. Make sure that you have enough insurance to meet your needs in this order: income protection; lump sum or instalment-term life insurance; private medical insurance; and critical illness insurance.

18. Ensure you complete a written nomination for your chosen beneficiaries in respect of your pension death benefits.

19. Make sure you have a will and Last Power of Attorney to ensure your wishes are carried out in the event of your death or mental incapacity.

20. Talk about money in your family, friendship circles, and workplace by discussing money challenges, how to be good with money (such as the ideas in this book) and what really matters in life and the role of money. You'd be amazed how liberating it can be to shine light on the truth.

American radio speaker and author Earl Nightingale said 'Never give up on a dream just because of the time it will take to accomplish it. The time will pass anyway.'

Remembering the concepts and ideas in this book and taking the time to work on the actions above will help to improve your financial well-being.

As a result you'll worry less about money, experience less stress, enjoy life more and live *your* dream.

Do let me know how you get on by visiting my website at www.jason-butler.com as I'd love to hear your story.

Namaste.

FURTHER READING AND RESOURCES

BOOKS

The Financial Wellbeing Book: Creating Financial Peace Of Mind by Chris Budd. LID Publishing, 2016.

Sheconomics: Add Power To Your Purse With The Ultimate Money Makeover by Karen J. Pine and Simonne Gnessen. Headline, 2009.

The One-Page Financial Plan: A Simple Way To Be Smart About Your Money by Carl Richards. Penguin Random House UK, 2015.

The Number: What Do You Need For The Rest Of Your Life, And What Will It Cost? By Lee Eisenberg. First Free Press, 2007.

Who Can You Trust About Money? By Paul Claireaux. Irate Investment ltd., 2013.

Enough?: How Much Money Do You Need For The Rest Of Your Life? By Paul D. Armson. CreateSpace Independent Publishing Platform; 1 edition, 2016.

How Much Can I Spend in Retirement?: A Guide to Investment-Based Retirement Income Strategies (The Retirement Researcher's Guide Series), by Wade Pfau, Retirement Researcher Media, 2017.

Left-Brain Finance for Right-Brain People by Paula Ann Monroe. Sourcebooks, Inc., 1998.

Mind Over Money: The Psychology Of Money and How To Use It Better by Claudia Hammond. Canongate Books Limited, 2016.

Your Money and Your Brain: Become A Smarter More Successful Investor, The Neuroscience Way by Jason Zweig. Souvenir Press Ltd., 2007.

The 3 Simple Rules of Investing: Why Everything You've Heard About Investing Is Wrong – And What To Do Instead by Michael Edesess, Kwok L. Tsui, Carol Fabbri and George Peacock. Berrett-Koehler Publishers, Inc. 2014.

Smarter Investing 3rd edn: Simpler Decisions for Better Results (Financial Times Series) by Tim Hale. FT Publishing International; 3 edition, 2013.

The Little Book of Common Sense Investing: The Only Way to Guarantee Your Fair Share of Stock Market Returns (Little Books. Big Profits) by John C. Bogle. John Wiley & Sons; Updated and Revised edition (7 Dec. 2017).

The Little Book of Bahavioral Investing: How Not to Be Your Own Worst Enemy by James Montier. John Wiley & Sons, Inc., Hoboken, New Jersey, 2010.

DIGITAL RESOURCES

Boring Money – www.boringmoney.co.uk

Describes itself as 'like the lovechild of a financial magazine and TripAdvisor'. Wide range of helpful information and insights on personal finance, explained in a simple and straightforward way.

Financial Well-being – www.financialwell-being.co.uk

Blogs, podcasts and other information on a range of personal financial well-being issues. Companion website to The Financial Well-being book.

Maven Adviser – https://www.mavenadviser.com

Blogs, podcasts, and calculators on personal finance presented by financial planner Andy Hart.

Meaningful Money – https://meaningfulmoney.tv

Blogs, videos and podcasts on a range of personal finance issues, presented in a highly accessible and friendly way by experienced financial adviser Pete Matthew.

Monevator – monevator.com

Personal blogs about 'money: making, saving, growing, and sometimes even spending it.' written anonymously by *The Investor* and *The Accumulator* for the non-expert.

Mr Money Mustache – www.mrmoneymustache.com

US focused personal finance insights and information written in a humourous tone

Paul Claireaux – paulclaireaux.com

Personal financial insights for non-financial people who want to be more confident and capable making financial decisions, written by ex financial services marketing executive Paul Claireaux.

REFERENCES

1 Rath, Tom, and Jim Harter. *Wellbeing: The Five Essential Elements*, Gallup Press. 2010.

2 *Financial Well-Being: The Goal of Financial Education*, Consumer Financial Protection Bureau (01/2015), p18 http://files.consumerfinance.gov/f/201501_cfpb_report_financial-well-being.pdf (accessed 17.10.17)

3 Ibid, p19

4 Momentum UK Household Financial Wellness Index 2017 Summary Report https://www.momentumgim.co.uk/wps/wcm/connect/mgim2/3a6e04d0-4d20-47f9-b1e2-26ed81db67bb/Final+summary+report+-+Financial+Wellness+2017.pdf?MOD=AJPERES (accessed 21.10.17)

5 Thaler, Richard, and Cass Sunstein. *Nudge*. London: Penguin Books, 2009. p45-46

6 Ajzen, Icek. 1991. "The Theory of Planned Behaviour." *Organisational Behaviour and Human Decision Processes* 50:2: 179-211.

7 Frank, R. H. 2004. "How not to buy happiness." *Daedalus* 133, 69-79.

8 Van Boven, L., M. C. Campbell and T. Gilovich. 2010. "Stigmatizing materialism: on stereotypes and impressions of materialistic and experiential pursuits." *Personality and Social Psychology Bulletin* 36: 551-563.

9 Solnick, Sara J, and David Hemenway. "Is More Always Better?" *Journal of Economic Behavior & Organization*, Nov. 1998 http://www.dl.icdst.org/pdfs/files/64d27b6bd5694361593729862f6a35bf.pdf (accessed 02.11.17)

10 Adapted from '£30K in debt: But finally, we're sorting it out.' Mirror Online 3 Feb 2012 http://www.mirror.co.uk/money/personal-finance/30k-in-debt-298585 (accessed 30.1017)

11 *Stuck in debt: Why do people get trapped in problem debt?*, Citizens Advice, (2017). https://www.citizensadvice.org.uk/Global/CitizensAdvice/Debt%20and%20Money%20Publications/Stuck%20In%20Debt.pdf (accessed 31.10.17)

12 'She's paid the mortgage for seven years, so why did the Co-op try to repossess this woman's home?' *Manchester Evening News* 14.06.17 http://www.manchestereveningnews.co.uk/news/greater-manchester-news/shes-paid-mortgage-seven-years-13187328 (accessed 31.10.17)

13 Families and households in the UK: 2016, Office for National Statistics

14 Aviva Family Finances Report Winter 2016/17: Living together – do the finances add up for cohabiting couples? https://www.aviva.com/content/dam/aviva-corporate/documents/newsroom/pdfs/newsreleases/2003/6882_Aviva_Family_Finance_Report_Winter_2017_secured_Wc2kyib.pdf (accessed 02.11.17)

15 Living together and marriage: legal differences, Citizens Advice https://www.citizensadvice.org.uk/family/living-together-marriage-and-civil-partnership/living-together-and-marriage-legal-differences/ (accessed 01.11.17)

16 Newcomb, Sarah. *Loaded: money, psychology, and how to get ahead without leaving your values behind*, Hoboken, NJ: John Wiley & Sons, 2016, p104

17 McGagh, Michelle. *The No Spend Year: How you can spend less and live more*, Coronet, 2017. You can also hear Michelle tell her story at https://www.youtube.com/watch?v=vRudjyOcub0

18 Lisjak, Monika, et al. "Perils of Compensatory Consumption: Within-Domain Compensation Undermines Subsequent Self-Regulation." *Journal of Consumer Research*, vol. 41, no. 5, 2015, pp. 1186–1203. *JSTOR*, www.jstor.org/stable/10.1086/678902. (accessed 30.10.17)

19 Newcomb, Sarah. *Loaded: money, psychology, and how to get ahead without leaving your values behind* Hoboken, New Jersey, John Wiley & Sons, Inc., 2016, p116

20 ibid.

21 Taken from http://kerririchardson.com/

22 The Money Charity http://themoneycharity.org.uk/money-statistics/ (accessed 19.09.17)

23 Nunes, J.C. & Boatwright, P. (2004) "Incidental Prices and Their Effect on Willingness to Pay". *Journal of Marketing Research*, XLI, 457-466.

24 ibid.

25 KPMG, *Global Automotive Executive Survey 2017* https://assets.kpmg.com/content/dam/kpmg/xx/pdf/2017/01/global-automotive-executive-survey-2017.pdf (accessed 28.10.17)

26 Szapiro, Aron, HelloWallet, *How much should workers save for emergencies?* 2015 http://info.hellowallet.com/rs/hellowallet/images/HelloWallet%20-%20How%20Much%20Should%20Workers%20Save%20For%20Emergencies.pdf (accessed 02.11.17)

27 Diacon, Stephen., Nurul Shahnaz and Ahmad Mahdzan. 2008. "Protection Insurance and Financial Wellbeing – A Report for the Financial Services Research Forum" University of Nottingham. https://nottingham.ac.uk/business/businesscentres/crbfs/documents/researchreports/paper55.pdf (accessed 25.09.17)

28 Stroke Association, 2017, *State of the Nation* https://www.stroke.org.uk/sites/default/files/state_of_the_nation_2017_final_1.pdf (accessed 21.10.17)

29 For an overview of this theory see Kahneman, D. (2012) *Thinking, Fast and Slow*. London: Penguin

30 Harter, James K., and Raksha Arora. 2010. "The Impact of Time Spent Working and Job Fit on Well-Being around the World." In Ed Diener, John F. Helliwell and Daniel Kahneman, eds, *International Differences in Well-Being*, 398-435. Oxford: Oxford University Press.

31 Clarke, Andrew E. 2010. "Work, Jobs, and Well-Being across the Millennium." In Ed Diener, John F. Helliwell and Daniel Kahnerman, eds, *International Differences in Well-Being*, 436-468. Oxford: Oxford University Press.

32 City & Guilds. 2012. http://www.cityandguilds.com/news/November-2012/careers-happiness-index-2012#.WYtwM3eGOYU (accessed 9.08.17).

33 Goldstein, Robin, et al, *"Do more expensive wines taste better? Evidence from a large sample of blind tasting."* American Association of Wine Economists, Working paper No. 16, April 2008

https://timedotcom.files.wordpress.com/2015/05/aawe_wp16.pdf (accessed 27.10.17)

34 Plassmann, H, J. O'Doherty, B. Shiv, A. Rangel, *"Marketing actions can modulate neural representations of experienced pleasantess"* https://www.ncbi.nlm.nih.gov/pubmed/18195362 (accessed 29.10.17)

35 Plassmann, Hilke & Bernd Weber, "Individual Differences in Marketing Placebo Effects: Evidence from Brain Imaging and Behavioral Experiments", *Journal of Marketing Research*, 2015 https://timedotcom.files.wordpress.com/2015/05/plassman_jmr_13_0613.pdf (accessed 29.10.17)

36 Whillans, Ashley V., Elizabeth W. Dunn, Paul Smeets, Rene Bekkers, and Michael I. Norton. "Buying Time Promotes Happiness", *Proceedings of the National Academy of Sciences of the United States of America* 114, no. 32 (August 8, 2017). (Pre-published online.) http://www.pnas.org/content/early/2017/07/18/1706541114

37 Gilovich, T. & Kumar, A. (2015). "We'll always have Paris: The hedonic payoff from experiential and material investments", In M. Zanna and J. Olson (Eds.), *Advances in Experimental Social Psychology*, Vol. 51 (pp. 147-187). New York: Elsevier.

38 Matz, Sandra C., Joe J. Gladstone and David Stillwell "Money Buys Happiness When Spending Fits Our Personality". *Psychological Science* Vol 27, Issue 5, pp. 715 – 725

39 Moll, Jorge, Frank Krueger, Roland Zahn, Matteo Pardini, Ricardo de Oliveria-Soza, and Jordan Grafman. 2006. "Human fronto–mesolimbic networks guide decisions about charitable donation" http://www.pnas.org/content/103/42/15623.abstract (accessed 07.11.17)

40 *When More is Less : Rethinking Financial Health*, Morningstar (2017) http://images.mscomm.morningstar.com/Web/MorningstarInc/%7Bb87a29d4-9264-4e6f-a5d7-5e65f8714f92%7D_US_ADV_MoreLess_Whitepaper_Final.pdf (accessed 06.11.17)

41 Hershfield, Hal. "Future Self-Continuity: How Conceptions of the Future Self Transform Intertemporal Choice", *Annals of the New York Academy of Sciences* 1235, no. 1 (2010): 30-43

42 Oeppen, J. and Vaupel, J., "Broken Limits to Life Expectancy", *Science* 296 (5570) (2002): 1029-31.

43 Financial Well-being Podcast: Redefining "Goals" With Carl Richards (9/03/17) http://www.financialwell-being.co.uk/2017/03/09/episode-15-redefining-goals-with-carl-richards/ (accessed 22.09.17)

44 Rohwedder, Susann, and Robert J. Willis. 2010. "Mental Retirement", *Journal of Economic Perspectives*, 24(1): 119-38.

45 Wu C, Odden MC, Fisher GG, *et al* "Association of retirement age with mortality: a population-based longitudinal study among older adults in the USA", J *Epidemiol Community Health* 2016;70:917-923. http://jech.bmj.com/content/70/9/917 (accessed 20.10.17)

46 Demographic Components of Future Population Growth: 2015 Revision, United Nations http://www.un.org/en/development/desa/population/theme/trends/dem-comp-change.shtml (accessed 06.11.17)

47 Gratton, Lynda., and Andrew Scott. *The 100-Year Life*, Bloomsbury, 2016, p2

48 Bogle, John, C. *Common Sense on Mutual Funds: New Imperatives for the Intelligent Investor*, John Wiley & Sons; Anniversary edition, 12 Jan. 2010

49 Doeswijk, Ronald Q., Lam, Trevin and Swinkels, Laurens. "Historical Returns of the Market Portfolio", 01.06.17 https://papers.ssrn.com/sol3/papers.cfm?abstract_id=2978509 (accessed 24.10.17)

50 "The Great Multi-Asset Fund Guide: The Gravy Train", Finalytic, 2017 https://finalytiq.co.uk/research-papers/ (accessed 09.11.17 – Paywall)

51 https://www.fourgenerationsoneroof.com/

52 Vanderbilt, Arthur T. *Fortune's Children: The Fall of the House of Vanderbilt*, Michael Joseph Ltd, 1990; Burden, Wendy, *Dead End Gene Pool : A memoir*, Avery Publishing Group, 2011.

53 Williams, Roy. & Vic Preisser. *Preparing Heirs: Five Steps to a Successful Transition of Family Wealth and Values* Robert D. Reed Publishers, Oregon, 2012.

ABOUT THE AUTHOR

Jason Butler is a Chartered Fellow of the Personal Finance Society and the Chartered Institute for Securities and Investment. He was a financial adviser for 25 years, 17 of which was as senior partner of the firm which he founded, until he retired from financial services aged 46.

Jason writes about personal finance for the Financial Times and Money Marketing and has appeared on BBC Radio, Sky News and other media outlets. He is an expert on financial well-being and personal finance capability and is a sought after keynote speaker and consultant.

Jason lives with his wife, two daughters, two dogs and a horse in rural Suffolk, UK.

 @jbthewealthman

www.jason-butler.com

Printed in Great Britain
by Amazon